Managing Digital Rights
a practitioner's guide

Managing Digital Rights
a practitioner's guide

edited by

Paul Pedley

facet publishing

© This compilation: Paul Pedley 2005
   The chapters: the contributors 2005

Published by
Facet Publishing
7 Ridgmount Street
London WC1E 7AE

Facet Publishing is wholly owned by CILIP: the Chartered Institute of Library and
Information Professionals.

First published 2005

British Library Cataloguing in Publication Data
A catalogue record for this book is available from the British Library.

ISBN 1-85604-544-7

Typeset from editor's disks by Facet Publishing in 11/14pt New Baskerville and
MicroSquare.
Printed and made in Great Britain by MPG Books Ltd, Bodmin, Cornwall.

Contents

The contributors

Sandy Norman is a freelance copyright consultant and, until recently, Copyright Adviser to CILIP. She has been involved with copyright matters for 14 years and has written many articles and presented papers both nationally and internationally on copyright issues. For several years, Sandy was the Secretary of the Libraries and Archives Copyright Alliance (LACA), and was also a member of other major committees on copyright including the EBLIDA Experts Copyright Group and the IFLA Committee on Copyright and other Legal Matters. From 1992 to 1996, she was the Copyright Adviser to IFLA, where she represented IFLA at major meetings of the World Intellectual Property Organization.

Paul Pedley is Head of Research at the Economist Intelligence Unit. He is a member of the Libraries and Archives Copyright Alliance, and is on the strategic advisory board of the JISC Legal Information Service. Paul regularly runs training courses on copyright, data protection and freedom of information, as well as on internet topics such as the invisible web and business information.

Helen Pickering is Copyright Manager for HERON (a division of Ingenta). She has been involved in providing digital course readings for students since her involvement with eLib's pioneering SCOPE project in 1997, and has been responsible for obtaining the necessary permissions for online and paper course packs since 1998. She currently manages HERON's copyright clearance service for approximately 80 universities and colleges, involving over 1500 rights holders. She has written various articles about the subject, and presents regularly on the topic.

Linda Purdy is Senior Information Adviser (Media Service) at Sheffield Hallam University. She manages the copyright clearance service for the University, advises University teaching staff and students on copyright issues relating to use of third-party materials, and has responsibility for administering the CLA, ERA, OU, NLA and DACS licensing schemes. Linda has presented papers on copyright as it affects higher education, and also on re-use of materials in the digital environment. She has acted as project manager on several multimedia development projects, with particular responsibility for advising on copyright matters. Linda is a member of the British Universities Film and Video Council Executive Committee.

Ian Watson has more than 20 years' experience in information management within specialist information services. He has worked extensively with traditional online information sources and also with the web since the first browsers appeared around 1993. His encounters with the internet in the early 1990s resulted in several articles and presentations on the emerging 'great electronic information bazaar' and for several years he contributed a monthly column to *Managing Information*. Currently he is Head of Rights and Information with Newsquest Media Group's Glasgow newspapers: *The Herald*, *The Sunday Herald* and *The Evening Times*. His responsibilities include licensing newspaper content (words and pictures) for use on websites, corporate intranets, books, magazines, digital archives, etc. He is also undertaking an LLM in IT and Telecommunications Law by distance learning from the University of Strathclyde.

Table of statutory material

Note: all legislation listed governs UK practice

Statutes

Statutory instruments

European directives

Treaties and conventions

Table of cases

Figures and case studies

Figures

Case studies

Abbreviations

ABC	Audit Bureau of Circulation
ADA	Australian Digital Alliance
ALCC	Australian Libraries Copyright Committee
ALCS	Authors' Licensing and Collecting Society
ASCAP	American Society of Composers, Authors and Publishers
BAPLA	British Association of Picture Libraries and Agencies
BUFVC	British Universities Film and Video Council
C&IT	communications and information technology
CCC	Copyright Clearance Center
CDPA	Copyright, Designs and Patents Act 1988
CED	Committee for Economic Development
CILIP	Chartered Institute of Library and Information Professionals
CLA	Copyright Licensing Agency
CORRA	Copyright and Related Rights Act 2000
DACS	Design and Artists Copyright Society
DAM	digital asset management
DeCSS	Decrypt CSS
DfEE	Department for Education and Employment (now the Department for Education and Skills)
DMCA	Digital Millennium Copyright Act
DOI	digital object identifier
DPS	Digital Permission Service
DRM	digital rights management
DRMS	digital rights management systems
DVD	digital versatile disc (or digital video disc)
EBLIDA	European Bureau of Library Information and Documentation Associations

ECCS	Electronic Course Content Service
ECJ	European Court of Justice
ECUP	European Copyright Users Platform
EEA	European Economic Area
ERA	Educational Recording Agency
EU	European Union
FE	further education
FEI	further education institution
GATT	General Agreement on Tariffs and Trade
HEFCE	Higher Education Funding Council for England
HEI	higher education institution
HERON	[was] Higher Education Resources On-Demand
HMSO	Her Majesty's Stationery Office
HTML	hypertext markup language
ICOLC	International Coalition of Library Consortia
ICSU	International Council for Science
IFLA	International Federation of Library Associations and Institutions
IFRRO	International Federation of Reproduction Rights Organisations
IPA	International Publishers Association
IPR	intellectual property rights
ISBN	international standard book number
ISP	internet service provider
ISSN	international standard serial number
JISC	Joint Information Systems Committee
LACA	Libraries and Archives Copyright Alliance
NESLI	National e-Journals Initiative (originally National Electronic Site Licence Initiative)
NGO	non-governmental organization
NLA	Newspaper Licensing Agency
OU	Open University
PA	Publishers Association
PDF	portable document format
TLTP	Teaching and Learning Technology Programme
TPS	technical protection system
TRIPS	Trade-Related Aspects of Intellectual Property Rights

UNESCO	United Nations Educational, Scientific and Cultural Organization
URL	uniform resource locator
USC	United States Code
UUK	Universities UK
VCR	video cassette recorder
VLE	virtual learning environment
WATCH	Writers, Artists and Their Copyright Holders
WCT	WIPO Copyright Treaty
WIPO	World Intellectual Property Organization
WPPT	WIPO Performances and Phonograms Treaty
WTO	World Trade Organization
WWW	world wide web

Preface

Information professionals are becoming increasingly reliant on content in digital form such as databases, news feeds, e-books, electronic reference materials or e-journals. They may also wish to digitize content that they hold in hard-copy format.

Rather than relying exclusively on copyright law in order to protect their content, rights holders make use of licences or contractual agreements – and also technology in the shape of digital rights management (DRM) systems and electronic rights management information systems – in order to protect and enforce their rights over digital assets. DRM technology is used to control access to digital content and the uses made of it, to obtain payment for it, and to ensure the integrity of the work. The Copyright Directive implemented in the UK through the Copyright and Related Rights Regulations 2003 gave legal protection to rights holders using such systems.

This book is intended for practitioners working in library and information centres, archives or museums who want to know whether they can digitize their collections, and if so how to get the rights to do so. It has been written in order to provide a practical guide to the use of digital content. It deals with the question of how electronic information can be used legitimately, outlines the issues to be considered and suggests practical ways in which copyright clearance can be obtained while keeping the administration to a manageable level.

Disclaimer

Paul Pedley and the other contributors to this book are not lawyers and they are not able to give legal advice. The contents of this book are intended to raise awareness of key digital rights management issues affecting information professionals, but the book does not constitute authoritative legal advice and should not be relied upon in this way.

1 Setting the scene

Paul Pedley

Introduction

Copyright gives the creators of a wide range of material – literature, art, music, sound recordings, films and broadcasts – economic rights enabling them to control use of their material in a number of ways, such as by making copies, issuing copies to the public, performing, showing or playing the work in public, or communicating the work to the public. It also gives authors a number of moral rights, including the right to be identified as the creator of certain kinds of material, and to object to distortion or mutilation of it.

Copyright does not, however, protect ideas unless these have been encapsulated in the form of a 'work' such as a book or a journal article. Nor does copyright protect such things as individual names, headlines, bibliographic citations or URLs (although a collection of them could potentially be protected by database right and/or copyright).

In the UK, and even more so in the USA, copyright is viewed as a property right, as a trading system for works of the mind which is designed to achieve a fair economic return for the creator of the content. Indeed, there seems to be a perception that stronger copyright protection generates new wealth for the country. The Geneva Declaration on the Future of WIPO (Consumer Project on Technology, 2004) which was signed by a wide range of organizations such as the International Federation of Library Associations and Institutions (IFLA), the American Library Association, and the Special Libraries Association as well as individuals such as Lawrence Lessig and Berndt Hugenholtz states: 'WIPO needs to enable its members to understand the real economic and social consequences of striking a balance between the public domain and competition on the one hand, and the realm of property rights on the other.'

The Declaration says that humanity faces a global crisis in the governance of knowledge, technology and culture which manifests itself in a number of ways, such as:

- Technological measures designed to enforce intellectual property rights in digital environments threaten core exceptions in copyright law for disabled persons, libraries, educators, authors and consumers, and undermine privacy and freedom.
- Private interests misappropriate social and public goods and lock up the public domain.

Indeed, the Declaration calls for a treaty on access to knowledge and technology. The use of digital rights management systems seems to be less about incentives or compensation than about control.

Digital rights management systems protect intellectual property rights. They are primarily used in order to control access to works as well as to control payment. But they can also be used to control the use and integrity of the work.

Unless specifically stated, this chapter refers to UK law. The implementation of the European Copyright Directive (2001/29/EC) through the Copyright and Related Rights Regulations in October 2003 heralded a number of far-reaching changes to copyright law. In view of these significant changes to copyright law, it is important for readers to ensure that they consult up-to-date guides to copyright which take account of the changes. These include Sandy Norman's *Practical Copyright for Information Professionals: the CILIP handbook*, Tim Padfield's *Copyright for Archivists and Users of Archives* and Graham Cornish's *Copyright: interpreting the law for libraries, archives and information services*. (All three of these titles are published by Facet Publishing.)

Of particular significance for this book is the fact that the Copyright and Related Rights Regulations set out the legal framework within which digital rights management systems are administered. They provide legal protection for technical measures and also for electronic rights management information.

The Regulations confirm existing rights of reproduction and

distribution or sale, and they give a new exclusive right of communication to the public for rights holders, as well as introducing a number of new criminal offences including one for by-passing or eliminating 'technological measures' or rights management information.

Why is digital different?

Access to hard-copy material tends to operate under a business model that differs from that for electronic information. In the hard-copy world you are normally able to buy a book or an issue of a periodical, and you then become the 'owner' of that book or journal part, even though you don't actually 'own' the rights to the content within it. This would usually entitle you to consult the publication whenever and wherever you please at no additional cost. You would also be perfectly at liberty to lend it to a friend, or to sell your copy second-hand.

The electronic world is, however, somewhat different. Instead of 'owning' the publication, you are merely 'leasing' it for a limited period of time under a licence agreement. You are, in effect, paying for the right to access the content under terms and conditions that are set out in the licence or contract. Rights holders are able to exert continuing control over every subsequent act of gaining access to the content of a work. Producers had previously been unable to control the private usage of their work once sold when this was in 'hard-copy' form. Reference here to the 'electronic world' is intended to cover digital information, and this includes everything in machine-readable form including digitized images, e-mails, websites, e-books, electronic journals and online databases.

Electronic information is protected by copyright. There is a common misconception in the case of the internet, for example, that because so much of the information on the internet is both readily available and free of charge that this somehow gives people an implied licence to copy. That is certainly not the case. Nor can you assume that if electronic information does not display the © symbol it is therefore in the public domain and can be copied freely. Indeed, the Copyright and Related Rights Regulations (SI 2003/2498) made the position clearer by introducing the new right of communication to the public. This is an exclusive right of the author as first owner of the copyright which covers electronic transmission of the work. If you were to publish to your website content in which you did not own the copyright you would be infringing the author's exclusive right to communicate the work to the public and this could potentially lead to a two-year prison sentence.

Many corporate websites have a legal notice which includes a statement on copyright; or they might even have a dedicated copyright notice. If you wish to copy material found on a website, you should check if there is a copyright statement on the site and, if so, whether this gives you the permission that you require. If it does not, or if there is no copyright statement on the site, it is advisable to contact the webmaster.

A single web page could contain many different copyrights. For example a textual article is protected as a literary work; graphics, charts or photographs as artistic works; a sound file as a musical work; and the HTML coding and metadata as a literary work. Each of these component parts of the website is protected. In addition, the website is protected by the right of communication to the public. Many websites also qualify for database right protection.

Database right

A key case on database right is that of British Horseracing Board Ltd and others vs William Hill Organization Ltd [2001] EWCA Civ 1268 (31st July, 2001).

The British Horseracing Board (BHB) maintain a database of registered horses, their owners and trainers, details of jockeys and fixture list of information. The BHB database is constantly updated. Indeed, the continuing cost of obtaining, verifying and presenting the contents of the database is of the order of £4 million a year, involving around 80 staff and extensive computer software and hardware. The database contains details of over a million horses. It consists of some 214 tables, containing over 20 million records. An estimated total of 800,000 new records or changes to existing records are made each year.

Initially, BHB won a high court challenge against William Hill over the use of pre-race data, arguing that internet bookmakers who wished to use information such as runners and riders should pay a copyright fee. Then, in May 2002, the Court of Appeal decided to refer a number of questions concerning the interpretation of the Database Directive to the European Court of Justice (ECJ) (case C-203/02). The judgment was published in November 2004, and this gives a better understanding of how the legislation is to be interpreted. The judgment came as a complete surprise to people because it overturned the previous findings, and said that William Hill had not, after all, infringed database right.

The court made clear that in order to attract Database Right protection a person has to show that there has been a qualitatively or quantitatively substantial investment in the obtaining, verification or presentation of the database contents; and that when making this assessment any investment in the creation of the data itself should be ignored. Applying this to the BHB case means that the significant effort involved in compiling lists of horses running in races – and verifying the information – does not count towards satisfying this test because the verification of the contents of the database take place at the stage of creation of the data.

In the physical world, access to a product requires a physical act which can generally be monitored or charged for. It might, for example, involve use of a photographer or a scanning machine. As such it is not easy to copy works on a large scale because the process is slow and cumbersome, and the quality of the resulting copies is poor. However, where content is already available in digital format, it is so easy to make a copy of a digital work that there is really no physical barrier to access, and piracy is therefore difficult to prevent. Digital materials differ from hard-copy materials in that they are easier to copy; the quality of the copy is much higher; the work can easily be copied to many other people; and the unit cost of the copying is much lower.

How rights holders protect their interests

Rights holders such as magazine and book publishers, music companies and producers of computer games or software are – understandably – concerned about their works being available in electronic form. Consequently, where their content is available in digital form, they are much more protective of it and a number of them will enforce their rights more aggressively. They want to prevent their digital content from being used, duplicated and distributed without authorization or compensation.

Some people have argued the case for copyright to be redefined and extended in order to provide protection to the creators of the work. In fact, rights holders have actually pursued a several-pronged approach in order to control access to and usage of their material. Indeed, many of the recent changes in copyright law have come about as a result of pressure from the entertainment industry in the form of major music, software and media corporations.

Strengthening of copyright law

One tactic has been to argue the case for copyright law to be strengthened. An example of this is where the period of copyright protection has been extended. In Europe this increased from 50 to 70 years after the death of the author (*post mortem auctoris*). Another example is the narrowing of copyright exceptions, such as fair dealing for the purposes of research or private study, and library privilege. In both cases the exception now covers only research or private study which is for a non-commercial purpose. Section 29(1) of the Copyright, Designs and Patents Act 1988 (CDPA) now reads:

> Fair dealing with a literary, dramatic, musical or artistic work for the purposes of research for a non-commercial purpose does not infringe any copyright in the work provided that it is accompanied by a sufficient acknowledgement.

With regard to the private study element, section 29(1c) of the Act does not explicitly state that this should be non-commercial:

> Fair dealing with a literary, dramatic, musical or artistic work for the purposes of private study does not infringe any copyright in the work.

However, it is not only implicit that 'private study' is always non-commercial, because section 178 of the CDPA, which is a section of minor definitions, does make it absolutely clear by saying that 'private study does not include any study which is directly or indirectly for a commercial purpose'.

Introduction of new protections

Another tactic has been to introduce new special protections. This happened with the Database Directive (96/9/EC). It was implemented in the UK through the Copyright and Rights in Databases Regulations (SI 1997/3032) which introduced the *sui generis* protection for databases. The definition of a database given in the Regulations is 'a collection of independent works, data or other materials that are arranged in a systematic or methodical way and are individually accessible by electronic *or other means*' and as such it covers both electronic and some hard-copy content. In order for a database to qualify for copyright protection, the contents of the database must be original. The test is that they must constitute the author's own intellectual creation by reason of the selection or arrangement of the contents of the database. Meanwhile, in order for a database to qualify for database right, substantial investment must have taken place in obtaining, verifying and presenting the contents of the database. Some databases qualify for both copyright protection and database right protection. However, even if a database does not qualify for copyright protection because its contents do not have sufficient originality, the database might still qualify for database right protection.

Use of technology to control access

Yet another tactic has been to use technology in order to control access to copyright materials including digital rights management systems. Rights holders may well feel that there are practical problems in policing the world wide web. Pursuing and catching those who have disobeyed copyright laws can be both onerous and time-consuming, and many copyright owners look towards technological solutions as a much better alternative to litigation because it enables them to actually prevent unlawful use of their online content before it occurs, rather than having to resort to litigation after the event.

Use of contract law

Rights holders also use the law of contract in order to protect their interests. Use of digital works is often subject to a set of terms and conditions in the form of a contract or licence agreement, and use of the material is therefore governed by the law of contract. This is significant because contract law is able with very few exceptions to override copyright law, so that copyright law does not apply. It means that, while it has taken years to develop a body of copyright legislation, all the hard work and negotiation to achieve a balance between the competing interests are usurped at a stroke by rights holders who require users to sign a licence agreement on their terms before they can make use of their digital products. There are only a couple of instances where the legislation stipulates that contract law cannot override copyright law. One of the few places where the legislation does do this appears in the Copyright and Rights in Databases Regulations 1997. Regulation 19(2) states:

> Where under an agreement a person has a right to use a database, or part of a database, which has been made available to the public in any manner, any term or condition in the agreement shall be void in so far as it purports to prevent that person from extracting or re-utilising insubstantial parts of the contents of the database, or of that part of the database, for any purpose.

According to the European Commission's April 2004 proposals on the management of copyright and related rights (Commission of the European Communities, 2004):

> DRMs do not present a policy solution for ensuring the appropriate balance between the interests involved, be they the interests of the authors and other rightsholders or those of legitimate users, consumers and other third parties involved (libraries, service providers, content creators . . .) as DRM systems are not in themselves an alternative to copyright policy in setting the parameters either in respect of copyright protection or the exceptions and limitations that are traditionally applied to the legislature.

However, in spite of what the European Commission says DRM systems in combination with licensing agreements are used by rights holders as a means of achieving an alternative to copyright policy; and one which is overwhelmingly in their favour. Indeed, the Royal Society (2003) stated that 'the ban on circumvention of technical protection measures . . . gives the owners in effect a perpetual right beyond the term of copyright without appropriate and/or effective fair dealing provisions. The shift is in effect to perpetual property rights rather than a social contract.'

Enforcement

A European Commission Directive of 2004 (2004/48/EC) deals with the enforcement of intellectual property rights through sanctions and remedies. The Directive requires all member states to apply effective, dissuasive and proportionate remedies and penalties against those engaged in counterfeiting and piracy and to create a level playing field for right holders in the EU. Once the Directive has been implemented – and this is required by 29 April 2006 – all member states will have a similar set of measures, procedures and remedies available for rights holders to defend their intellectual property rights if they are infringed.

Under the Directive, member states will have to appoint national correspondents to co-operate and exchange information with other member states and with the Commission. As well as benefits for rights holders, the Directive contains appropriate safeguards against abuse, ensures the rights of the defence and includes references to the protection of personal data and confidential information.

Negotiating licences

It would be dangerous for anyone to assume that they could get out of a contract on the grounds that it was unfair. While it is true to say that there is legislation such as the Unfair Contract Terms Act 1977 and the Unfair Terms in Consumer Contracts Regulations (SI 1999/2083), people should bear in mind that the courts are reluctant to interfere in contractual relationships where each party has freely entered into a contract. The courts work on the assumption that each party enjoys reasonably equal bargaining power, and that they enter into an agreement with their eyes open. However, the Unfair Contract Terms Act does provide some protection for licensees, such as where a clause is deemed to be void on the grounds that it contains an unreasonable exclusion of liability.

A contract clause is not invalid purely on the basis that the licensee did not read that particular clause when they signed the contract; so buyers need to read through the contract terms very carefully. Similarly, if there are terms which the buyer does not understand they should take advice from a lawyer on what the contract actually means, because the terms still apply whether or not the buyer understands them.

Under the terms of a licence, the copyright owner as licensor grants the licensee a number of rights to do certain restricted acts in return for paying a fee. Licensees are often required to accept very restrictive terms and conditions. For example, the contract may well exclude permitted acts or copyright exceptions such as fair dealing. If this is the case, then the information professional should ensure that the rights are preserved by asking to have inserted into the agreement a paragraph stating that 'This agreement is without prejudice to any acts which the licensee is permitted to carry out by the terms of the Copyright, Designs and Patents Act 1988 and nothing herein shall be construed as affecting or diminishing such permitted acts in any way whatsoever.'

Information professionals have to negotiate the terms under which digital assets can be used and this can be a time-consuming activity. In some instances no negotiation of contract terms is possible, for example where there is a 'click-use' or 'shrink-wrap' licence. From the point of view of the information professional, having a lot of different licence agreements can be problematic because it is not easy to remember all of the contractual obligations if the wording of each contract is different. Librarians have to summarize the key points of the contracts as succinctly as possible so that they are then able to communicate the licence terms to their end users.

Model licence agreements

The time involved in negotiating deals for electronic products can be considerable. That, combined with the logistical problems of complying with a number of differently worded terms and conditions, has led to a number of initiatives towards model licence agreements with standardized terms. For example:

- John Cox Associates (www.licensingmodels.com) has drawn up a series of model contracts for public, academic and corporate libraries.
- The International Coalition of Library Consortia (ICOLC) produced a statement of current perspective and preferred practices for the selection and purchase of electronic information (ICOLC, 1998). Primarily aimed at the higher education community, the statement was updated in December 2001.
- The European Copyright Users Platform (ECUP) has produced four model licences for public libraries, national libraries, university libraries and company libraries. These contain clauses favourable to libraries.
- The NESLi2 model licence for journals is based on the NESLI and PA/JISC model licence for journals.
- The Zwolle Principles (www.surf.nl/copyright) set out a fair basis for copyright relationships between authors, publishers and universities. A copyright toolkit is being developed as a collection of aids to finding the right model or solution for an institution's particular situation.

Finally, rights holders may try to use other types of intellectual property law such as patent law or trademark law in order to protect their intellectual property.

What is meant by 'digital rights management'?

The Publishers Association (2004) argues that the phrase 'digital rights management' is often used to cover two very distinct concepts; and as a result the whole subject has become highly politicized. It separates out the different elements involved:

- Management of digital rights where market-enabling technology is used in order to identify and describe a piece of content,

which includes information about the rights and permissions attached to it
- Digital management of rights which involves the use of technical protection measures, including encryption, access and copy control mechanisms that are designed to ensure that certain usage rules are complied with. Rights holders 'wrap' a set of rules around content in order to define how control can be manipulated and shared by the purchaser of the copyrighted or premium content.

Richard McCracken in a communication to the editor, suggests a third definition of digital rights management: using a back-office system to manage the information associated with a collection of licensed assets – so that a library for example, could use DRM in order to manage the licences by which it has subscribed to e-journals, etc. The Open University is developing such a system in order to manage the information it holds on licences, contracts, rights holders' addresses, payments details, etc.; in this way it can manage its collection of imbedded third-party content in course materials and audiovisual and broadcast programmes.

Technical aspects of digital rights management systems

Key elements of digital rights management systems are:

- identifiers, such as digital object identifiers – numbers or codes permitting the unique identification of a piece of content
- metadata – information about the piece of content which may include, for example, the identity of the rights holder, the price for using the work, and any other terms of use.

Mechanisms for controlling access to digital works include:

- security and integrity features of computer operating systems such as traditional file access privileges
- rights management languages (such as Rights Expression Language) which express in machine-readable form the rights and responsibilities of owners, distributors and users to enable the

computer to determine whether requested actions fall within a permitted range
- encryption allowing digital works to be scrambled so that they can be unscrambled only by legitimate users
- persistent encryption permitting the buyer to use information while the system maintains it in an encrypted form
- digital watermarks which add a small amount of information to the work which identifies the work and cannot easily be removed. They are used by rights holders who wish to keep track of any copying and distribution of their digital works. Watermarks embed information, such as information about ownership, into a digital work in much the same way that a piece of paper can carry a watermark
- fingerprinting algorithms which take a little piece of the information which identifies the work, although the work itself is not affected.

Charles Oppenheim (2001), writing about the Copyright Directive (2001/29/EC) states that 'there is no question that the directive shifts the law quite significantly in favour of rights holders and against users'.

Legal protections for digital rights management systems
Legislation supporting DRM systems

Technical measures such as digital rights management systems are criticized by those who wish to access the material without permission where they feel that 'fair dealing' entitles them to copy a limited amount – the so-called 'technological lock-up'. The technical measures now have the force of law behind them, and it is a criminal offence to circumvent such a measure. Legislation at national and international level supports the use of digital rights management systems. It includes:

- the WIPO Copyright Treaty (Article 11)
- the WIPO Performances and Phonograms Treaty (Article 18)
- Directive 2001/29/EC on the Harmonization of Certain Aspects of Copyright and Related Rights in the Information Society (Article 6)

- the Copyright and Related Rights Regulations 2003, implementing the Copyright Directive (2001/29/EC) in the UK (section 296)
- the Digital Millennium Copyright Act, passed by the USA government in 1998
- the Australian Copyright Amendment (Digital Agenda) Act 2000.

For a more detailed look at international developments in legislating for digital rights management systems, see Chapter 2).

DRM systems and the copyright exceptions

Rights holders are deploying digital rights management systems in order to control usage of their digital assets. Lawrence Lessig (quoted in *The Economist*, 15th July 1999) writes that software could replace legal code – in other words that digital rights management systems could override copyright law. A number of commentators have argued that the legally enforceable access controls are rendering worthless the permitted acts or copyright exceptions, and, in the USA, annulling the 'first sale doctrine'. Indeed, some American observers go so far as to say that the Digital Millennium Copyright Act is therefore unconstitutional. The 'first sale doctrine' entitles the owner of a lawfully made copy to sell it, lend it or give it away without the consent of the copyright owner. It is codified into US legislation as section 109 of the US Copyright Act.

Now that legislation protects the use by rights holders of technical protection measures it follows that, even if you believe that a copyright exception entitles you to copy a limited amount of a work, you are not able to enjoy that right if the work is protected by a technical protection measure: the act of breaking through that measure in order to make the copy is an offence. Strictly speaking, if you know how to access the content and are quite sure that you are entitled to have access for fair dealing purposes, you could go ahead. But you are not able to pass on that knowledge to anyone else, because that would be an offence. And the problem with fair dealing is that you can never be absolutely sure that a court would agree that what you had done was indeed fair. This begs the question as to what legal remedy is available to a lawful user who is prevented from circumventing 'technical measures' in order to make the copy they require and which, because it relies on one of the copyright exceptions (such as fair dealing), does not infringe copyright.

The answer is that under the Copyright and Related Rights Regulations (2003) a complaint can be made to the Secretary of State for Trade and Industry where an 'effective technological measure' does not allow copyright exceptions or permitted acts as set out in the CDPA to be exercised. Following an investigation the Secretary of State may give a direction to the owner of the rights in the work requiring them to ensure that the complainant can benefit from the permitted act. It should be noted, however, that this applies only where no suitable licensing scheme is available.

Laurence Kaye (2003) quotes US consumers on the Digital Millennium Copyright Act which implements the WIPO Copyright Treaty in the USA: 'current rules are the logical equivalent of executing all of the residents of a town to make sure you get the one serial killer among them'. It does not address the standards needed to make the legal provisions on DRM work.

Managing rights

Digital rights management systems are frequently seen only as a technical protection measure – a technical means of enabling rights holders to deliver digital content in a controlled way – preventing users from having access to the content unless they meet the requirements of the rights holder, be it financial or otherwise, and preventing users from using the accessed content in ways other than the rights holder has given permission for. This viewpoint is too narrow, because DRM systems should also take account of the management of those rights; and provide functionality such as verifying the authenticity of information, indicating if it comes from the source claimed and if it has been altered – whether inadvertently or fraudulently. The Copyright and Related Rights Regulations make it a criminal offence to interfere with or remove electronic rights management information – which means information provided by the rights holder that identifies the work, the author or any other rights holder, or information about the terms and conditions of use of the work. In a sense these provisions strengthen the author's moral right to be identified as the author of the work.

Libraries are involved in the clearance and management of rights, and a properly managed introduction of DRM systems, in its widest sense, has the potential to assist information professionals in managing their services by including DRM, access management, contract management and management of the clearance process within such a system.

Balancing the needs of creators and users

In many respects, the protection of intellectual property rights in electronic materials has been seriously considered only in the last ten years or so. This has been concurrent with the increasing availability of materials in electronic formats, which has, in turn, been largely triggered by the exponential growth of the world wide web, and the simultaneous increase in the electronic availability of content.

Protection is typically conceived of in legal and technical terms, determined by what the law permits and what technology can enforce. Graham Cornish (2003) says that 'extensive research has shown that it is not possible to teach a computer to distinguish between a use which should be paid for and one that should not'. Protecting digital content requires a multifaceted approach comprising a mix of technology, consumer education and the law. Technology provides means, not ends; it can assist in enforcing intellectual property policy, but it cannot provide answers to social, legal and economic questions about the ownership of and rights over works, nor can it make up for incompletely or badly answered questions.

It seems as if the legislation is being driven by the technology and its limitations whereas the development of DRM systems should be driven by the principles behind the legislation, especially with regard to the ability to benefit from exceptions.

Successful DRM systems balance a number of competing demands such as fair compensation for the creators of digital content alongside the rights of end users to access and use information. Getting the balance right is not easy to achieve. If a system is so heavily protected that it makes it difficult for a legitimate user to access the content, then this will damage potential sales. Equally, if the system provides only a basic level of protection which can easily be circumvented, then that too would clearly threaten the level of business.

Technology

The first concern of any DRM solution should be to make sure that the intended user of the content does not experience any constraint on the legitimate use of the content they have acquired; and the second concern is that people who do not have such rights are prevented from accessing the content. The reality, however, is that DRM technologies often confront legitimate users of digital content with inconvenience and needless restrictions in their attempts to prevent those without the required rights to the content from gaining access.

DRM systems aim to automate the process of licensing works and of ensuring that licence terms are complied with. In order to achieve this, there is a rights model at the heart of all DRM technology. Rights models are schemes for specifying the rights to content that a user can obtain in return for some consideration, such as registration, payment or allowing their use of the system to be tracked.

Typically, content is encrypted: in order to get the decryption key a user must pay money, provide an e-mail address, agree to their usage being tracked or take some other action along similar lines. DRM systems enforce a set of business rules according to the conditions that are laid down by content owners in respect of the use of the content which is protected by intellectual property. These rules typically concern such questions as:

- Who is entitled to access a work?
- At what price?
- On which terms? For example, the terms address questions such as:
  - whether a user is entitled to make copies of the work
  - how many copies can be made
  - for how long a user is entitled to access a work
  - whether a back-up or archive file can be created
  - whether a user can make changes to the work
  - whether a user can access the work on one or on multiple devices.

The Commission of the European Communities (2004) recognizes the need for DRM systems and services to be interoperable in order to avoid any problem of incompatibility:

The establishment of a global interoperable technical infrastructure on DRM systems based on consensus among the stakeholders appears to be a necessary corollary to the existing legal framework and a prerequisite for the effective distribution and access to protected content in the Internal Market.

Privacy issues

The consumer wishes to be anonymous, in the same way as they would be when buying a book or going to see a film. However, when they obtain digital access to a work, some sort of identity 'trail' is needed in order to prevent unauthorized copying. This leads to a conflict of interests between consumers on the one hand, who do not want to have any invasion of their privacy, and rights holders on the other, who want to track the usage of their products.

DRM systems trace an individual user's usage of materials, which incorporates personal data. In order to protect an individual's privacy records which are kept should not be held any longer than is necessary to trace a use and get payment. After that the records should be stripped of their identifiers and kept purely for statistical purposes. This prevents a cumulative record of one or more users' activities from being created.

In their April 2004 proposals *The Management of Copyright and Related Rights in the Internal Market*, the European Commission expresses concern about the ability of DRM systems to trace the user's behaviour (section 1.2.5, para 2) and says that the user's privacy should be preserved (section 1.2.5, para 8).

Obtaining copyright clearance

In an ideal world, information users would like to have information delivered to their desktop through a single portal where they are required to enter only one user id and password. They also want the content to be available through a user-friendly search interface which should be available to them even when they are on the move. Users want to have access to both the latest material for current-awareness purposes, and an archive of older content. They want access both to titles and to the full text, or at the very least to informative abstracts.

Users also want to be able to disseminate the content to anyone, and to annotate and amend materials – something which impinges upon an author's moral rights. Since we are talking about a utopian world, users want all of this at no cost to themselves or indeed their employers.

The problem is that this is the publisher's nightmare scenario, and librarians find themselves caught in the middle. On the one hand, they have to respect the intellectual property rights of the content providers; on the other hand, they have to provide access to content for their users. The digital library cannot come about until these legal problems are resolved.

If what we want to communicate digitally is not already available in a digital format, then there is a need to digitize the content. This requires the user – often via an information professional – to get copyright clearance.

The permissions process

The permissions process can be broken down into a number of component parts:

1 Receive the customer's request.
2 Check the bibliographic details are correct.
3 Establish whether clearance is required – this might require legal expertise.
4 Trace the copyright owner.
5 Request copyright clearance.
6 Chase up the request where necessary.
7 If permission is granted, a set of terms and conditions is likely to be attached. If not, there may be a need to negotiate those terms.
8 Notify the customer of the outcome.
9 Get the approval of the customer to go ahead at the agreed rate, and on the agreed terms.
10 Pay the copyright fee to the rights holder.

Licences covering digital copying offered by the collective licensing societies

In the UK, neither the Copyright Licensing Agency (CLA) nor the Newspaper Licensing Agency (NLA) has licences covering content that is born digital. However, they do have ones which permit the digitization of content from hard copy into digital format under carefully defined conditions.

These licences are more restrictive than for hard-copy content. The repertoire covered will not be as extensive. For example, in the case of the CLA, the material that can be digitized is limited to UK content. Or, in the case of the NLA, newspapers may have chosen not to give a mandate to the NLA to license the digitization of their content, as is the case with News International. Another factor is that the period of time that electronic content may be retained could well be more restrictive. In the case of NLA, for example, digital copies used to disseminate cuttings by e-mail or on an intranet can be held for up to seven days only, after which they must be destroyed.

In order for librarians to make a copy of material for their users which is subject to copyright protection, they have a number of options:

- Get copyright clearance directly from the rights holder.
- Take out a licence from someone who acts on behalf of the rights holder, such as a collective licensing society.
- Make use of one of the copyright exceptions or permitted acts.
- Pay for a copyright cleared copy through a licensed document supply service.
- Pay a copyright fee by using the CLA sticker scheme.

Having a copyright-fee-paid copy does not necessarily allow you to make further copies. For a more detailed look at the process of obtaining the necessary permissions, see Chapter 3.

Permitted acts/copyright exceptions

A primary infringement of copyright occurs when a person exercises one of the rights holder's exclusive rights without their permission or consent. The rights – which are set out in section 16 of the CDPA include:

- the right to copy the work
- the right to issue copies of it to the public
- the right to rent or lend the work to the public.

Berne three-step test

The Berne Convention of September 1886 for the protection of literary and artistic works enables national legislatures to provide a number of copyright exceptions or permitted acts, so long as they meet a three-step test, and:

- apply only in certain cases
- do not conflict with a normal exploitation of the work or other subject matter
- do not unreasonably prejudice the legitimate interests of the rights holder.

The permitted acts or copyright exceptions therefore make it possible for users of copyright works to undertake a limited amount of copying without having to get the permission of the copyright owner, so long as the copying is done under the conditions set out in the legislation. The permitted acts are, by definition, a lawful use of a work even though they have not been authorized by the publisher. They provide an invaluable counterbalance to the rights holder's exclusive rights in the wider interests of research, scholarship and culture.

The exceptions provide better safeguards for the public interest than can reliance on licensing, which is naturally monopolistic, often idiosyncratic and only available to those who can afford it.

An adapted form of the wording of the Berne three-step test appears in the Copyright Directive (2001/29/EC), and therefore any copyright exceptions are permissible only if they meet each of the elements of the three-step test.

Fair dealing

The best known of the UK's copyright exceptions is 'fair dealing'.

While not identical, there are similar provisions in the copyright laws of other countries – 'fair use' in the USA, or 'private copying' in continental Europe. Fair dealing allows an individual to make a copy of a limited amount of a work, without having to ask permission or pay fees. This would not entitle the user to copy all or a 'substantial part' of a work, because that would be an infringement of copyright.

The conditions set out in the legislation require the copying to be 'fair'. In order to meet this requirement, any copying should not damage the legitimate commercial interests of the copyright owner; and it must also be for one of the permitted purposes. To count as 'fair dealing' it must be copying for research or private study and not for a commercial purpose; undertaken for criticism or review, or for the purposes of reporting current events.

In the USA, people consider four key criteria – PNAM – in order to determine whether it is right to rely upon the fair use provisions:

- P – purpose
- N – nature
- A – amount or substantiality
- M – market impact.

In theory, fair dealing applies to electronic copying as well as photocopying. However, copyright owners are often very unhappy about electronic fair dealing. Publishers and rights owners have different interests to those of the user community, so it is not a given that they will find mutually acceptable solutions. However, one example of where they have worked together successfully is the *Guidelines for Fair Dealing in an Electronic Environment*, developed by the Joint Information Systems Committee (JISC) and the Publishers Association (1998).

Where DRM systems are employed, all uses of the work have to be with the publisher's permission. The act of circumvention, rather than any infringement of copyright, is criminalized.

Writing in *The Irish Times* (16 August 2002), Danny O'Brien makes a number of pertinent comments: '. . . while there are plenty of punishments for consumers who dare break the locks on their possessions, there are very few legal controls to prevent publishers from walking all over fair dealing rights with the same locks'; on

Ireland's Copyright and Related Rights Act 2000, 'under CORRA-style laws, breaking copy protection to assert your existing fair dealing rights is illegal'.

It is important to point out that fair dealing is a defence. It is not a right and it does not provide any kind of guaranteed immunity against an action for copyright infringement. If you were faced with such an action, you would have to prove that the copying passed the Berne three-step test. The problem with fair dealing is that the legislation does not make it clear what is deemed to be 'fair'. Consequently, this has to be judged on the basis of each individual instance of copying, and no one can be absolutely sure that the copying is fair, unless it is deemed to be so by a court. Fair dealing is therefore a rather risky and unpredictable defence, because what is fair in the eyes of a user, may not be considered fair by the rights holder. There are no copying limits which can be said to be fair in all circumstances. Section 16 of the CDPA states that copyright is not infringed unless the whole or a substantial part of a work has been copied. While it is clear that the whole of a work has been copied or not, it is not so easy to determine whether or not a 'substantial part' has been copied, not least because the legislation does not define the phrase 'substantial part'. However, even though the legislation does not define what would constitute a 'substantial' part, it is nevertheless clear that this relates not just to quantity but also to quality.

Library privilege

Library privilege entitles library staff to copy items for their patrons and, so long as the conditions set out in The Copyright (Librarians and Archivists) (Copying of Copyright Material) Regulations 1989 are met, the member of library staff undertaking the copying is indemnified against any action being taken against them. The indemnity derives from the declaration form which must be signed by the user. Library staff are in a privileged position: in the UK the only other person guaranteed immunity against an infringement action is Her Majesty the Queen.

Business models

In order to ensure that a DRM solution will fit neatly with specific business needs, potential adopters of DRM technologies must consider the following:

1 **the type of content** to be controlled, because the cost of designing, developing and deploying the protection system has to be in harmony with the market for the content
2 **the value of the content** (to both provider and recipients) versus the cost of protecting it, because the cost of the protection should be kept in proportion to the value of the work being protected. For content that is inexpensive or already available in a reasonably priced, non-internet medium, there is no point in having an expensive technological protection system that drives up the price of internet delivery
3 **the life cycle** of the content to be controlled
4 **the specific rights** to be controlled for each content type
5 **usability** – a technical protection system (TPS) that is cumbersome and difficult to use may deter paying customers. If that happens, it is a failure, no matter how successful it may be at preventing theft
6 **appropriateness to the threat**. Preventing honest customers from giving copies to their friends may require nothing more than a reasonably priced product, a good distribution system, and a clear set of instructions. At the other end of the spectrum, preventing theft of extremely valuable content that must at some point reside in a networked PC requires a very sophisticated TPS, and even the best that is available with current technology may not be good enough.

Each of these considerations will help to bring the technical protection system in line with the business model.

Most business models for traditional copyrighted works involve the sale of a physical item that then becomes the property of the customer. The economics of the transaction include the costs associated with creating the initial content and first copy of the work and the costs of reproduction, marketing, distribution and other overheads. In this scenario, the costs associated with trying to recreate a physical copy of the work of equal quality to the original are relatively high. In the digital world, by way of contrast, the traditional business model is brought into question because of the considerably lower costs and effort involved in the reproduction and distribution of copies which are of the same quality as, and therefore indistinguishable from, the original.

Outline of following chapters

In the remaining chapters of this book, leading experts in the field expand upon these themes.

In Chapter 2, Sandy Norman sets the scene for how digital rights management has developed, by discussing the history of and politics behind international copyright agreements – such as the WIPO treaties.

In Chapter 3, Helen Pickering considers the processes involved in obtaining copyright clearance in order to convert print material into a digital format. The chapter asks whether clearance is needed, and describes how to find out who holds the rights, get hold of the rights holder's contact details and get the rights holder to grant permission, as well as some common terms and conditions. The chapter also covers the most common courses of action, and highlights some problems which may occur during the process. It ends by looking at a number of issues for requesting institutions.

In Chapter 4, Linda Purdy looks at the changes in teaching and learning, and the development of the digital learning environment. The chapter considers the digital rights management issues for tutors and students accessing and using resources created by someone else, and also considers ownership rights in newly created materials. It addresses the need for institutions to incorporate these digital rights management issues into their policies and the need for institutions to educate their employees and students. It concludes by considering how the need for access to third-party reusable resources can be met.

In Chapter 5, Ian Watson considers the perspective of the corporate rights holder in general while drawing on experience within newspaper publishing. Newspapers contain a variety of material – text, photographs, maps, diagrams, cartoons, etc. Reuse of this content, whether in electronic editions or by third parties – second rights – requires clarity with respect to copyright and moral rights ownership.

The chapter examines the factors and processes that need to be considered in the licensing process.

References

Berne Convention (1886) for the Protection of Literary and Artistic Works, September.

Commission of the European Communities (2004), Communication from the Commission to the Council, the European Parliament and the European Economic and Social Committee, *The Management of Copyright and Related Rights in the Internal Market*, COM (2004) 261 final, 16 April.

Consumer Project on Technology (2004) Geneva Declaration on the Future of WIPO, www.cptech.org/ip/wipo/futureofwipodeclaration.pdf [accessed 23 December 2004].

The Copyright and Rights in Databases Regulations SI 1997/3032.

The Copyright and Related Rights Regulations SI 2003/2498.

The Copyright (Librarians and Archivists) (Copying of Copyright Material) Regulations (SI 1989/1212).

Cornish, G. P. (2004) *Copyright: interpreting the law for libraries, archives and information services*, 4th edn, London, Facet Publishing.

Cornish, G. P. (2003) *Guidelines on the Recent Changes to Copyright Law*, London, Libraries and Archives Copyright Alliance and Museums Copyright Group.

Council directive of 14 May 1991 on the legal protection of computer programs (91/250/EEC).

Directive 96/9/EC of the European Parliament and of the Council of 11 March 1996 on the legal protection of databases.

Directive 2001/29/EC of the European Parliament and of the Council of 22nd May 2001 on the harmonization of certain aspects of copyright and related rights in the information society.

European Copyright Users Platform (ECUP) *Heads of Agreement for Site Licences for the Use of Electronic Products*. Sample licences are available for public libraries, national libraries, university libraries and company libraries, www.eblida.org/ecup/licensing [accessed 23 December 2004].

International Coalition of Library Consortia (ICOLC) (1998) *Statement of Current Perspective and Preferred Practices for the Selection and Purchase of Electronic Information*, www.library.yale.edu/consortia/statement.html [accessed 23 December 2004].

Joint Information Systems Committee and the Publishers Association (1998). *Guidelines for Fair Dealing in an Electronic Environment*, JISC/PA.

Kaye, L. (2003) *Digital Rights Management: the legal debate*, SCL Internet Interest Group Meeting, 26 March, www.laurencekaye.com [accessed 23 December 2004].

Lessig, L. (1999) Digital Rights and Wrongs, *The Economist* (15 July).

Norman, S. (2004) *Practical Copyright for Information Professionals: the CILIP handbook*, London, Facet Publishing.

O'Brien, D. (2002). Irish Can Lead Way to Fairer Deal on Copyright, *The Irish Times* (city edition), (16 August), 55.

Oppenheim, C. (2001) Reports on Developments Worldwide on National Information Policy, www.la-hq.org.uk/directory/prof_issues/nip/intellectual.htm [accessed 23 December 2004].

Padfield, T. (2004) *Copyright for Archivists and Users of Archives*, 2nd edn, London, Facet Publishing.

Publishers Association (2004) *Digital Rights Management – to avoid confusion*, www.publishers.org.uk [accessed 23 December 2004].

Royal Society (2003) *Keeping Science Open: the effects of intellectual property policy on the conduct of science*, www.royalsoc.ac.uk [accessed 23 December 2004].

The Unfair Contract Terms Act 1977.

The Unfair Terms in Computer Contracts Regulations 1999 SI 1999/2083.

WIPO Copyright Treaty – Article 11 covers obligations concerning technological measures, while Article 12 deals with obligations concerning rights management information.

WIPO Performances and Phonograms Treaty – Article 18 covers obligations concerning technological measures, and Article 19 relates to obligations concerning rights management information.

2 Digital rights management: an international perspective

Sandy Norman

Introduction

Arguably, one cannot discuss an international perspective of digital rights management (DRM) without alluding to copyright law and its implications for both rights holders and the users of their works. This chapter, therefore, concentrates mainly on the history of and politics behind international copyright agreements, the 1996 WIPO treaties, which set the scene for DRM to develop. A brief description of the implementation of these international treaties in Europe, the USA and Australia is also given. User and rights holder reactions are also given. This chapter does not cover types of DRM systems and technological protection devices such as encryption, watermarking, digital object identifiers and the like; these are covered in Chapter 1.

Digital rights are an extension of the economic rights given to creators under copyright law. Authors and creators are protected by copyright law against unauthorized reproduction, publication, distribution, etc. of their works. Copyright legislation does not treat digital works any differently from print-based material but, because of the ease of reproduction and communication to the public, the rights are usually *managed* differently. As well as digital rights and digital rights management, there are also digital rights management *systems*, i.e. systems to deal with the management of rights. To complicate matters even further, there is also the *technical protection* of digital rights by technical protection systems (TPS) and DRM systems.

Many other definitions have been used for DRM and DRM systems. For example, the World Intellectual Property Organization[1] (WIPO) says that '[t]he application of information technology to facilitate the exploitation of rights is commonly referred to as "digital rights management" (DRM)' whereas DRM systems (DRMS) are aimed at enforcing contractual conditions on use of content and so automating the licensing process.[2] The European Commission refers to DRM systems which can be used to clear rights, to secure payment, to trace behaviour and to enforce rights.[3] The UK Publishers Association (PA) maintains that there is a distinction between the management of digital rights and digital management of rights and that the two should not be confused. The PA says that the *management of digital rights* means market-enabling technology, i.e. 'the identification and description of a piece of content, including necessary information about the rights and permissions attached to it (with payment mechanisms if appropriate) packaged in such a way as to be "interoperable" '.[4] (International interoperable standards are still being developed.) Whereas *digital management of rights* means copyright protection technology, i.e. technical protection systems, such as anti-copying devices or tracking mechanisms.

Information revolution and copyright

With the advent of digital technology and the internet, the world became a global marketplace. The potential for content providers and rights holders to exploit their works beyond their normal markets expanded greatly. However, there were several obstacles to overcome. The major bottleneck affecting rights holders was lack of control in preventing unauthorized copying. Works could whiz around the world at the touch of a few buttons. The question was whether it was strictly legal from the copyright point of view and, in any case, were there mechanisms in place to prevent it. The answer to both questions was 'No'. Signing up to international copyright conventions was not compulsory. Many nations, therefore, did not have appropriate copyright legislation in place. Many nations ignored or even encouraged copying, regarding such activities as a way of developing creative industries. In the eyes of rights holders in the developed world this was piracy. The music and film industries, especially, were concerned about cloned copies of sound recordings and films, but publishers were also concerned about pirated editions of their works.

Rights holders became suspicious of all copying, whether legal or illegal. In the early to mid-1990s, obtaining authorization to make a digital copy using the normal permission-seeking channels was considered as potential for a loss of control over the item and could lead to piracy. Loss of control meant loss of income. This meant that any requests by librarians and information professionals to copy works as part of the normal library service, e.g. for preservation purposes or inter-library document supply, were met with an unequivocal 'No'. There was a major problem of lack of trust on the part of rights holders, particularly publishers. They could not be sure that librarians would not abuse any permission. Several scare stories were circulating in the UK at this time. One example was that if permission was given to a librarian to make a digital copy of a work then only one copy would ever be purchased because the librarian could make the copy available to every other librarian using the interlibrary loan system. Another was that the British Library would be able to put all its works in digital format and make them available using library privilege. Both stories were totally unfounded but, even so, they served to make authors and publishers even more reluctant to discuss the digitization of their works and increased the division between rights holders and users. Rights holders were unhappy about the use of copyright exceptions, especially any library privileges, and began to question whether digital exceptions were necessary at all. (See the 'digital is different' argument on page 42). Librarians and information professionals, fearing litigation, were equally apprehensive about copying digitally under an exception. In some countries, copyright law in the early 1990s appeared to permit the making of a digital copy, but any subsequent uses (e.g. storage for any length of time) required permission. So, even though the technology existed for the profession to provide an efficient service to users, librarians and information professionals were unable to take advantage because of uncertainty. The situation was wholly unsatisfactory for both sides.

International agreements

There was growing pressure for WIPO to help resolve the copyright problems caused by the impact of digital technology. Discussions on adopting new rights appropriate in the digital environment took place over several years. The World Trade Organization (WTO)[5] TRIPS agreement played a major part by establishing that all nations had to be brought into line with the principles enshrined in the Berne Convention on Copyright.[6] Nations had to adopt appropriate copyright laws and enforce them, otherwise they would be hit by trade sanctions. All nations, even developing ones, desiring to trade with other nations, have had to sign up and abide by TRIPS.

In May 1996, the WIPO discussions were concluded with the preparation of new treaties. Proposals for three new copyright treaties, drafted jointly by the European Commission and the USA, were received and discussed. They immediately became controversial for the user community and intermediaries. The strengthening of author and performer rights was at the expense of adequate user privileges. The three treaties on the table for adoption were on copyright, on the rights of performers and phonogram producers and on the protection of databases. However, because of lack of time the discussion on databases was deferred and is still the subject of discussion at the WIPO Standing Committee.

New rights were added in the proposed instruments. Among these were:

- a communication to the public right to prohibit unauthorized transmission by any telecommunication method
- legal protection against circumvention for technical protection measures and digital rights management systems.

Also proposed was a definition of the reproduction right to include 'direct and indirect reproduction whether permanent or temporary, in any manner or form'. This was not adopted but was replaced by a partly agreed statement and a partly voted statement.

Article 11 of the WIPO Copyright Treaty requires signatory countries to provide adequate legal protection and effective legal remedies against the circumvention of effective technological measures used by rights holders to protect their works. Article 18 of the WIPO Performances and Phonograms Treaty places obligations on signatory countries in respect of technological measures used by performers or producers of phonograms.

Exceptions and the user lobby

Because of a strong lobby by consumer groups, mainly the International Federation of Library Associations and Institutions

(IFLA) and the European Bureau of Library Information and Documentation Association (EBLIDA), provision is made in these treaties for signatory nations to allow new exceptions and limitations in their copyright laws which are appropriate to the digital environment as well and affirms that existing exceptions apply to both the print and electronic environment. There were agreed statements to this effect. Article 10 states that:

(1) Contracting Parties may, in their national legislation, provide for limitations of or exceptions to the rights granted to authors of literary and artistic works under this Treaty in certain special cases that do not conflict with a normal exploitation of the work and do not unreasonably prejudice the legitimate interests of the author.

(2) Contracting Parties shall, when applying the Berne Convention, confine any limitations of or exceptions to rights provided for therein to certain special cases that do not conflict with a normal exploitation of the work and do not unreasonably prejudice the legitimate interests of the author.

Furthermore, the Agreed Statement to Article 10 clarifies this and allows scope for signatory nations to extend exceptions in the digital environment:

It is understood that the provisions of Article 10 permit Contracting Parties to carry forward and appropriately extend into the digital environment limitations and exceptions in their national laws, which have been considered acceptable under the Berne Convention. Similarly, these provisions should be understood to permit Contracting Parties to devise new exceptions and limitations that are appropriate in the digital network environment.

It is also understood that Article 10(2) neither reduces nor extends the scope of applicability of the limitations and exceptions permitted by the Berne Convention.[7]

It has been recognized that, despite rights holder pressure to reduce user privileges, the user coalition was successful in influencing the outcome of the 1996 WIPO diplomatic conference and the subsequent treaties and thus maintaining the copyright balance.

IFLA and EBLIDA, the only NGOs representing the user community, worked together to lobby. They wrote extensive briefing papers and gave them to each member. These papers drew attention to the shortcomings of the treaty language with regard to the need for access by users. The team, helped by the telecom industry which had its own agenda on liability of internet service providers (ISPs), lobbied hard to get exceptions and limitations recognized in the treaties. This was extremely important because authors and performers had a much stronger and tighter protection for their rights in the digital environment and this needed to be balanced with the needs of those who used their works. It was disappointing to have this success undermined by national interpretations of the treaties, especially by the European Union. The same battles were fought all over again while the EU Copyright Directive[8] was in passage and similarly in the USA with the Digital Millennium Copyright Act (DMCA).

Enforcement

The WIPO Copyright Treaty (WCT) and the WIPO Performances and Phonograms Treaty (WPPT) were both adopted in December 1996 and came into force in 2002 after 30 countries had ratified. Most of the major developed nations have still to ratify. Although the USA has ratified with the adoption of the Digital Millennium Copyright Act, the EU and Australia, along with most other nations in the world, have not. The EU cannot ratify until all its Member States have the appropriate legislation in place. To date (December 2004) 50 nations have ratified the WCT and 48 have ratified the WPPT.

E-commerce and the birth of DRM systems

The WIPO treaties are often referred to as the internet treaties because they address the issues surrounding protection for works on the internet and they have paved the way for e-commerce. They are seen to be innovative because they address directly the needs of authors and rights holders to protect their works in digital form by tackling the technological protection device issues. Prior to the WIPO diplomatic conference, Charles Clark, then General Counsel to the International Publishers Copyright Council and Copyright

Representative of the Federation of European Publishers, made a profound and oft quoted statement: 'The answer to the machine is in the machine.' The solution to the computer allowing copying lay in the computer itself:

> The ideal is a system which can undertake several different tasks, preferably all at the same time. A system must be able to identify copyright materials, to track usage, to verify users, and to record usage and appropriate compensation. In addition, the system should provide security for the integrity of the copyrighted material (freedom from tampering) and some level of confidentiality or privacy for the user. It might also provide the user with a price list showing various costs for different uses and individual materials along the model of a retail establishment.[9]

Arguably this was the inception of DRM systems. Sophisticated technological protection and management devices (TPS) could be put on digital works to prevent them being copied. All rights holders needed was the legal back-up to be able to detect and stop the use of circumvention devices as well as the dissemination of unauthorized digital copies.

Protection for TPS

Such legal back-up was granted by the WIPO treaties. Article 11 of the WCT and Article 18 of the WPPT, give legal protection to rights holders against circumvention of technical protection systems.[10] Article 11 of WCT states:

> Contracting Parties shall provide adequate legal protection and effective legal remedies against the circumvention of effective technological measures that are used by authors in connection with the exercise of their rights under this Treaty or the Berne Convention and that restrict acts, in respect of their works, which are not authorized by the authors concerned or permitted by law.

WCT Article 12 and WPPT Article 19 also protect rights management information. Article 12 of the WCT states:

(1) Contracting Parties shall provide adequate and effective legal remedies against any person knowingly performing any of the following acts knowing, or with respect to civil remedies having reasonable grounds to know, that it will induce, enable, facilitate or conceal an infringement of any right covered by this Treaty or the Berne Convention:

    (i) to remove or alter any electronic rights management information without authority;

    (ii) to distribute, import for distribution, broadcast or communicate to the public, without authority, works or copies of works knowing that electronic rights management information has been removed or altered without authority.

(2) As used in this Article, 'rights management information' means information which identifies the work, the author of the work, the owner of any right in the work, and any numbers or codes that represent such information, when any of these items of information is attached to a copy of a work or appears in connection with the communication of a work to the public.

Signatory nations to the WIPO treaties are obliged to provide adequate legal protection and effective legal remedies against unlawful circumvention of technical protection and rights management information systems. So, the challenge for national implementers would have to be one of trying to please both parties.

Interestingly, the language of the WIPO treaties regarding protection for technical protection systems was said to be suitably flexible to allow national governments to hammer out the details in their national implementations.[11] The controversial nature of national implementations indicates that the legislators thought otherwise.

In theory, with the adoption of the WCT and WPPT, the way was open for safe e-commerce. Rights holders could safely manage the digital rights of their materials by making them available online using various methods for recouping investment, e.g. licensing or pay-per-view, and the user community could rely on the accuracy of the information when making transactions. However, in reality, many rights holders, mainly in the entertainment industry, still had concerns about online piracy and the ease of hacking into and circumventing a technical protection regardless of its sophistication. Their fears were realized with the advent of file-sharing systems and the sharing of methods to circumvent protection devices, e.g. the case of the Decrypt CSS (DeCCS) code.[12]

Communication to the public right

Also of great importance to the management of digital rights was the adoption in the WCT and WPPT of a new right of communication to the public. Article 8 of the WCT states:

> . . . authors of literary and artistic works shall enjoy the exclusive right of authorizing any communication to the public of their works, by wire or wireless means, including the making available to the public of their works in such a way that members of the public may access these works from a place and at a time individually chosen by them.

There is similar wording in the WPPT covering audiovisual material and broadcasts. This is a right to communicate a protected work to the public by electronic transmission. This means putting works on to the internet where such works are available at any time for access; in other words, interactive access as opposed to fixed broadcast transmissions.

WIPO treaties: some implementations

All nations that signed up to the WIPO treaties had to adopt the new rights into their laws before they could ratify the treaties. A number of developed nations have updated or begun updating their copyright laws. The following is a brief overview of some of the controversy surrounding the implementation in the laws of three major areas: the European Union (EU), the USA and Australia.

European Union

Deliberations to agree the appropriate terminology in the EU Copyright Directive[13] regarding technical protection of digital rights took a very long time because of the controversy. Article 6 begins with the words 'member states shall provide adequate legal protection against the circumvention of any effective technological measures, which the person concerned carries out in the knowledge, or with reasonable grounds to know, that he or she is pursuing that objective'; and the Directive seeks to harmonize the legal protections against circumvention of effective technological measures and against provision of devices and products or services across the European Union.

Article 6.2 of the Directive requires member states to provide legal protection against the 'manufacture, import, distribution, sale, rental, advertisement for sale for rental, or possession for commercial purposes of devices, products or components of the provision of services' for the purposes of circumventing technological measures, including encryption, scrambling or other copy control mechanisms. The Directive states that if a technical protection device or system is employed to prevent access or copying then this may not be circumvented for unlawful purposes. For example, if a website prevents unauthorized access to the contents by some technical means, then it would be unlawful to interfere in order to circumvent such protection to gain access.

With regard to the issue of preventing lawful acts such as copying under an exception, the Directive encourages member states to promote voluntary agreements between rights holders and the users of copyright-protected material. If there are no such voluntary agreements, member states are allowed to 'take appropriate measures' to ensure that beneficiaries of an exception or limitation are able to benefit.[14] However, there is a nasty sting in the tail in that, if there is a contractual agreement in place, then member states are unable to take these appropriate measures. Many users believed that this would make such safeguards useless if contractual agreements covered non-negotiated contracts such as shrink-wrap or click-use licences.[15]

The introduction of the new Communication to the Public Right was not overly controversial and so largely acceptable to users as well as rights holders. Despite it not being adopted by the WIPO treaties, the EU also decided to define the Reproduction Right to include all transient and incidental copying.

The exceptions to the Right of Reproduction (Article 5.2) and the Rights of Reproduction and Communication to the Public (Article 5.3) caused the greatest concern. Apart from one mandatory exception,[16] member states were given the freedom to pick and choose which exceptions suited their laws provided they did not contravene the Directive conditions. However, if a member state did not already have certain exceptions,[17] then there was no provision given in the Directive to introduce any new ones. Member States could adapt only existing ones to fit the Directive. The Directive conditions were extremely restrictive and constrained many member states. Copying and communicating to the public was restricted directly or indirectly to non-commercial purposes which meant that any copying for the purposes of education or research tainted by any monetary gain was not allowed. Rights holders could also expect compensation whenever their works were copied and used even if the uses benefit the community. Exceptions, largely accepted for many years by governments, rights holders and users alike, were now seen to be unlawful.[18] For the user representatives, having fought hard at WIPO to preserve the exceptions and to obtain provision for them to be extended into the digital environment, this came as a major blow.

Implementation of the Copyright Directive in Europe is still in progress. Not all member states have legislation in place. Some countries are still in the process of negotiation with rights holders and users. The way each country[19] has interpreted and implemented Article 6 with regard to fair practice exceptions is very interesting. For example:

- In Finland, consumers are experiencing difficulties with copy-protected CDs but there appears to be no provision in the draft legislation to allow circumvention for private use.
- In Germany, the situation is similar. If a TPS is attached to a work then private copying is null and void. However, the law says that any copy protection material has to be identified and clearly labelled with a name and a postal address so that action may be taken to have the work made available to the purchaser. There are criminal sanctions if not.
- In Denmark, one may circumvent a work which is not protected by law, i.e. public-domain material. Also it is not illegal for a user to circumvent a system if the (sole) purpose is to make use of a work which has been lawfully acquired. For example, a user may use the DeCCS code to view a DVD on a Linux platform. There are

safeguards in place to allow users to benefit from exceptions: if a rights holder has been requested to make a work available for a purpose covered by an exception (other than private copying), this has to take place within four weeks otherwise users may circumvent the TPS themselves. This presumes that the user is technically capable of circumventing, of course. Any disputes are dealt with by the courts.

- The Netherlands has safeguards similar to those in the UK: in the absence of any voluntary agreements between rights holders and users, the government can take action. Consumers requested that a logo be placed on material protected by a TPS but this was not accepted by the legislators.

- French CD-ROM producers have been using copy protection technology on their products. For some consumers this has meant that they have been unable to listen to legally purchased products because the TPS prevents it. Some cases have been brought to court to try resolve the problems but many cases are still pending. The relevant area of law is commercial law which states that consumers have a right to information about a product and a right to be able to use the product they buy, otherwise the product can be judged defective.[20]

The USA

The US Digital Millennium Copyright Act 1998 (DMCA)[21] was equally controversial and angered the library profession. It gives copyright protection to creators and providers of digital content and outlaws the creation of devices or products that can circumvent digital watermarking, encryption and other technologies used to prevent pirating or other forms of copyright infringement.

The main issue for US librarians was how to preserve the principle of 'fair use' when works are locked up by technology. Fair use is similar to the UK CDPA fair dealing provision, allowing limited access to copyright-protected works for specific purposes, but it is different in that specific uses are not outlined. The argument for fair use access was similar to that in the UK and Europe: if access to works is protected by technological measures, how can the public exercise fair use with regard to those works? As a result of heavy lobbying, libraries and non-profit educational institutions were given a very limited 'browsing right' to circumvent a technical protection measure in order to evaluate a work before purchasing or licensing. However, once the review was completed, the work could not be accessed again. The question still remained unanswered about how a library could obtain the means to circumvent the technical measure, if the librarian is unable to purchase any equipment in order to circumvent, because the selling of equipment is prohibited under the ban on infringing devices. This was also a question raised in Europe. Unlike in Europe, no specific safeguards were proposed, but Congress agreed to review any adverse effects of the legislation after a specified time.[22]

A report by the US Digital Connections Council of the Committee for Economic Development (CED)[23] was issued in March 2004. This recognized the dilemma that the incorporation of any fair use into a DRM system is impossible. A work is either protected against unlawful access or it is not. There appears to be no middle way. The report deduces that DRM systems may prevent what has previously been viewed as legitimate access to information, for example, criticism: 'No DRM scheme we know can simultaneously protect against unauthorized uses and allow individual overrides whenever the user feels that what he or she is doing is reasonable.' US librarians may take comfort from the fact that at least this has been recognized, but the solution has not been identified, although the report does recommend that consumers should be involved in evaluation and approval of any government-mandated technological protection systems in order to achieve some balance.

Many believe that the DMCA has failed because it has not been effective at preventing piracy in cyberspace. All it has achieved is to stifle harmless and even beneficial uses of material for research and teaching.[24] In an attempt to counter the fair use/no circumvention dilemma caused by the DMCA, a new piece of legislation has been proposed in 2004. Called the Digital Media Consumers' Rights Act,[25] it would remove some restrictions on bypassing the security that prevents illegal duplication of DVDs, some CDs and software. It has the backing of librarians, liberal consumer groups and some technology firms but is opposed by the entertainment industry and the Business Software Alliance. If adopted, the Act would allow consumers to make copies of legally purchased material for 'fair use' purposes even if this meant circumventing any copy-protection measures. Selling copied material or any other form of copyright infringement would remain illegal, of course.

Australia

The Copyright Amendment (Digital Agenda) Act 2000[26] is Australia's legislation to implement the WIPO treaties. It updates the Copyright Act 1968 to take account of technological developments such as the internet and pay TV. Despite the arguments from copyright owners that 'digital is different', the drafters set out to strike essentially the same balance between owners and users of copyright as existed immediately prior to the amendments. To librarians and information professionals in Europe and the USA, this was refreshing. The Explanatory Memorandum, for example, states: 'as far as possible, the exceptions replicate the balance struck between the rights of owners and the rights of users that has applied in the print environment'. When compared with the language of the EU and US legislation, it is therefore seen to be extremely well balanced. This is mainly due to successful campaigning by the Australian Libraries Copyright Committee (ALCC) and the Australian Digital Alliance (ADA). In Australia, it is not an infringement for libraries, archives, museums and galleries to make digital copies of material in their collections for preservation and internal management purposes and to use such copies on intranets for staff use, subject to certain safeguards. Another difference between the UK and Australia is that the Australian legislation makes collective licensing in educational establishments statutory and the Digital Agenda Act has extended these licences to the online environment.

Regarding the WIPO provision to protect technical protection and rights management systems, like the EU and US solutions, these appear to fall far short of what librarians wanted. Australia introduced a limited set of exceptions for permitted purposes to resolve the problem of legitimate access to works protected by such systems. The drafters of the Australian Digital Agenda Act declined to prohibit use of a circumvention device or service. Instead, the Act prohibits certain commercial dealings in circumvention devices. A 'qualified person' may lawfully manufacture, import or supply circumvention devices for permitted purposes. These permitted purposes are: library/archive reproduction and communication, reverse engineering of computer programs, educational copying, parliamentary copying and government copying. Australian librarians believe that these anti-circumvention provisions represent an unacceptable extension of the power of rights holders to control access as well as reproduction of their works by effectively increasing the reach of copyright protection to non-infringing uses such as fair dealing and uses in relation to insubstantial parts of a work. It is maintained that, if a work is protected by a technological protection measure, no user will be able to access (let alone copy) even an insubstantial portion of that work, unless they fall within one of the very few exceptions which will enable them to legitimately obtain a circumvention device.[27]

Rights holders vs users

It is important to understand that the chequered history of digital rights management is partly due to the lack of trust which has developed between rights holders and users, mainly from the education and library community. Both sides had a lot to lose. Here are some of the arguments and fears.

The 'digital is different' argument

During the latter part of the 1990s, with the potential to gain the maximum return on investment by licensing digital works, there was a growing trend by rights holders to erode traditionally recognized exceptions by claiming that digital is different. As digital copies can be made of works without any loss of quality, at the touch of a key, these copies can be rapidly transmitted to multiple users or downloaded in their entirety. This potential loss of control and income led to a vigorous lobbying campaign by rights holders, including authors and artists, but most notably by publishers and media companies. Some publishers and reproduction rights organizations, for example, were claiming that the old system of having exceptions and limitations to copyright was anachronistic and should no longer apply to future copyright legislation. In 1996, a representative from the International Federation of Reproduction Rights Organisations (IFRRO) was reported as saying that in the analogue world library privileges were generally equated with free use, in the sense that no authorization was required and no remuneration paid and that it could not be assumed that such privileges should continue to apply in the digital environment: 'RROs, authors and publishers all agree that in the digital environment free uses, including library privileges, need to be carefully considered. Analogue privileges are not transferable as such to the digital environment'.[28] If librarians are given exceptions in the digital environment, they could download copies and circulate them around the world using interlibrary loan! Exceptions were also unnecessary as permission could easily be obtained. This belief led to the original narrow language of the draft proposals for the WIPO treaties and in the first two drafts of the EU Copyright Directive, and was also behind the original draft text of the US DMCA.

While recognizing that there were additional problems faced by rights holders in protecting their works, librarians, as the user representatives, argued that the principle of having exceptions which are in the public interest for the benefit of research, education, etc. was still valid. In 1996, they were supported by the WIPO treaties with the agreed statements which said that contracting parties could make provisions for new exceptions in the digital environment as well as recognizing that existing exceptions fully applied to the digital environment. However, post WIPO, librarians have had to lobby even harder to prevent the narrowing of fair practices, especially library copying.

Some progress was reached in 2001, although rather belatedly, with the publication of a joint statement from the Joint Steering Group of the International Federation of Library Associations and Institutions (IFLA) and the International Publishers Association (IPA). Both parties finally agreed to resolve this argument and issued a joint press release:

> While the fundamental principles underlying copyright protection in the print environment remain the same in the electronic environment (in this sense, 'digital is not different'), the Group recognises that the advent of new technologies has fundamentally changed methods of publication and dissemination as well as rights management (in this sense, 'digital is different').[29]

The important point made in the press release is that the 'fundamental principles' of copyright which include exceptions and limitations have been acknowledged and publicly accepted by publishers.

Technological lock-up fear

The problem of the coexistence of TPS and exceptions has proved too difficult to resolve. None of the national implementers of the WIPO treaties described above has been able to resolve this dilemma to the satisfaction of users. Users have long had concerns about the sophistication of these devices and their effect on access to knowledge. Such 'watertight' protection means that the only access to protected works has to be with permission or by licence only. Exceptions, of any kind, appear meaningless.

Copyright protects works for a specified period of time, not in perpetuity, for the reason that it must eventually be freely available to be enjoyed by all. However, digital technology has the potential to lock-up information included in works for ever. Such works will never become public domain. Such a locking-up of information therefore distorts the principles of copyright law enshrined in international conventions. The information is available, of course, but only to those few who can afford to pay for it. It will never be accessible to the many, for example to those in developing countries.

The fear of total control over information

Copyright law is designed to seek a balance between the legitimate interests of creators of works and the needs of users to have access to such works. It is in the public interest for laws to be flexible enough to allow access and use of works in specific cases. Copyright is designed to encourage creativity so that potential creators can research the works of others, without fear of prosecution, in order to develop new ideas.

The international library community believes the situation to be extremely ominous. IFLA is concerned that the increased use of licensing and technological protection is distorting the balance towards commercial interests and away from society's need for access because access to works can now be controlled by:

- copyright
- technological devices
- legal protection against circumvention of TPS
- contractual conditions.

An IFLA position paper states:

> The combination of protected technological measures and licenses can
> lead to an absolutely unlimited protection of the interests of the rights
> owners, who benefit from several cumulative layers of protection:
> copyright protection, technological protection, legal protection of the
> technological measures, and contract law.[30]

IFLA believes that the principle behind the exceptions is under threat
and the balance of power over information is tilting too far in favour
of major content providers and away from the general public interest.
Providing content is a multi-million dollar industry. Although users do
not have rights as such, there are certain rights to education and
freedom of expression belonging to society which are enshrined in the
Universal Declaration of Human Rights.[31] These 'rights' are under
threat. Even if there is a tiny exception window, it will always be so
carefully prescribed that users, i.e. librarians and information
professionals, fearing liability, will be far too cautious to take
advantage. The control of access to information in digital form means
control over a commodity which should benefit the greater good. The
irony is that the argument for greater copyright protection stems from
protecting individual authors' rights (creators) yet these rights (and
the arguments for them) are appropriated (and harnessed) by global
corporate entities and used against those who do the creating.[32] This is
the information rich versus the information poor argument.

This dilemma has since been acknowledged by WIPO. However, no
suggestions of how to resolve the issues have been put forward.
Instead, WIPO recognizes that the problem will occupy the minds of
the copyright industry and users and policy makers for some time![33]
The recent Committee for Economic Development (CED) report from
the USA also acknowledges that the consequences of providing legal
and regulatory quick fixes for protecting digital works are likely to
have a detrimental effect on innovation and economic growth. The

report recommends that time should be taken to build consensus between all parties in the information chain, including the users, before applying 'traditional legal safety valves'.[34]

The future: global management of rights

Rights holders are pushing for all uses of digital content to be authorized by permission or licence as part of a DRM system, but this should not be at the expense of upsetting the copyright balance between protection and access. Any imbalance will affect the ability of creators to create future works. DRM systems, according to the WIPO survey report, are generally welcomed by users and intermediaries as well as content providers as such systems *should* enhance legitimate access to digital works.[35] EBLIDA has stated that the focus of any DRM system should be on effective *management* rather than concentrating purely on *protection*.[36] A properly managed DRM system would assist a library in managing its rights clearance service and should be welcomed, says the UK Publishers Association, because the enabling technology used to manage rights should bring benefits to both rights holders and users alike by making it easier to use content. A DRM system should not be confused with copy protection technology.[37]

The need for standards

DRMs need to be standardized if they are to reach their potential as part of global digital licences and to be acceptable to users. The European Commission commissioned a report on digital rights management standardization following the adoption of the Copyright Directive 'with a view to identifying in that context the current status of DRM usage and possible means to ensure effective implementation of DRM in the marketplace'.[38]

The need for legislation on collective management of rights

In April 2004, the European Commission adopted a communication on the management of copyright and related rights. This states that EC legislation on the collective management of rights, and particularly on the governance of collecting societies, would be highly desirable. It also says that the development of DRMs should, in principle, be based on their acceptance by all stakeholders, including consumers, as well as on copyright policy of the legislature.[39] The report also recognizes that DRM systems should not be seen as 'an alternative to copyright policy in setting the parameters either in respect of copyright protection or the exceptions and limitations that are traditionally applied by the legislature'.[40]

Summary

The history of the international protection and management of digital rights has not had an easy passage. For rights holders, the world of e-commerce could function and develop more smoothly if copyright protection was total and there were no more annoying exceptions and user considerations to cope with. For the international library community and its users, the need to fight to maintain and extend the principle of exceptions and limitations to copyright in the digital environment has become even more important. The copyright balance between protection and access for legitimate purpose is in danger of becoming upset by the advance of digital technology and digital protection systems. In practice, almost all uses of works in digital form will always be with permission or licence because the need to copy and use these works is not covered by any kind of fair dealing or fair use exception. This is where global DRM systems need to be developed fairly, with both rights holder and user in mind.

Legal access to a work protected by a TPS remains a big problem demanding an international solution. For it to work at present, safeguards have to be in place and these must be workable. Circumvention of a TPS must be allowed if a legally purchased work is not accessible on the user's equipment. Failing that, there has to be a legal process, either described under copyright law or possibly under consumer law, which forces a rights holder to make the work available for a legitimate purpose. The use of a mandatory labelling system provided for in Germany, indicating on which platform(s) the work may be accessed, appears to be a sensible idea. Consumers then have the choice of whether to buy or not.

Notes and references

1 WIPO is the international body which, among other things, puts in place and manages international intellectual and industrial property conventions.
2 World Intellectual Property Organization (WIPO) (2002) *Intellectual Property on the Internet: a survey of issues*, www.wipo.int/copyright/ecommerce/en/pdf/survey.pdf [accessed 23 December 2004].
3 European Commission (2004) *The Management of Copyright and Related Rights in the Internal Market*, COM (2004) 261, www.europa.eu.int/comm/internal_market/copyright/documents/documents_en.htm [accessed 23 December 2004].
4 Publishers Association, *Digital Rights Management: to avoid confusion*, www.publishers.org.uk/ [accessed 23 December 2004].
5 The WTO is the international body which administers rules covering international trade. There are very few countries today that are not members of the World Trade Organization. The WTO oversees a number of agreements dealing with international trade, including the General Agreement on Tariffs and Trade (GATT). An important part of the WTO treaty system is the Agreement on Trade-Related Aspects of Intellectual Property Rights (TRIPS) which is intended to harmonize the intellectual property regimes of all member countries.
6 Norman, S. (2004) *Practical Copyright for Information Professionals: the CILIP guide*, London, Facet Publishing.
7 WIPO Copyright Treaty 1996.
8 European Council Directive on the Harmonization of Certain Aspects of Copyright and Related Rights in the Information Society (2001/29/EC).
9 Clark, C. (1996) The Copyright Environment for the Publisher in the Digital World, Joint ICSU Press/UNESCO Expert Conference on Electronic Publishing in Science, UNESCO, Paris, 19–23 February.
10 Paul Pedley explains the types of technical protection systems in Chapter 1 of this book.
11 *Intellectual Property on the Internet: a survey of issues*. Op. cit.
12 A young Norwegian boy decrypted a TPS on a purchased DVD because he was unable to play it on his computer. He wrote some

software called DeCSS to crack the code but also published the code on the internet for others to use. However, it was found that the code could be used to decrypt films as well as DVDs.

13 European Council Directive on the Harmonization of Certain Aspects of Copyright and Related Rights in the Information Society (2001/29/EC).

14 Ibid. Recital 51 and Article 6.4.

15 Shrink-wrap licences are called this because they are completely encased in a cling film and are purchased on a take-it-or-leave-it principle: if one buys the product and unwraps it, one is bound by the licence terms. If one does not agree to the licence terms, then the product may be returned to the vendor. Similarly, online access to certain websites is governed by the user agreeing up front to abide by the terms and conditions. If the user does not click to agree, then further access is denied. There is no other legal way of accessing the contents of such sites. Such non-negotiated licences are believed to be enforceable.

16 European Council Directive on the Harmonization of Certain Aspects of Copyright and Related Rights in the Information Society (2001/29/EC). Article 5.1 regarding the exception for temporary acts of reproduction which are transient and incidental and integral and essential to enable a transmission or a lawful use of the work.

17 France, for instance, had only a few minor exceptions in its copyright laws.

18 UK fair dealing, for example.

19 Brown, I., *Implementing the European Union Copyright Directive*, www.fipr.org/copyright/guide/index.htm [accessed 23 December 2004].

20 www.ipr-helpdesk.org/index.htm [accessed 23 December 2004].

21 Digital Millennium Copyright Act, Pub.L.No.105-304, 112 Stat. 2860(1998) (codified in scattered sections of 17 U.S.C.).

22 Norman, S. (2004) *Practical Copyright for Information Professionals*, op. cit.

23 Digital Connections Council of the Committee for Economic Development (2004) *Promoting Innovation and Economic Growth: the special problem of digital intellectual property*,

www.ced.org/docs/report/report_dcc.pdf [accessed 23 December 2004].

24 Vaidhyanathan, S. (2002) Copyright as Cudgel, *The Chronicle of Higher Education*, 2 August.

25 www.house.gov/boucher/docs/dmcra108th.pdf [accessed 23 December 2004].

26 Copyright Amendment (Digital Agenda) Act 2000, no.110 (Austrl.).

27 Flahvin and McLean (2001) *The Digital Agenda Act: how the new copyright law (and contract) is redefining the relationship between users and owners of copyright*, CyberLRes 21, www.austlii.edu.au/au/other/CyberLRes/ [accessed 23 December 2004].

28 ECUP, *Report on Steering Group Meetings with Rightholders*, www.eblida.org/ecup/docs/g1.htm [accessed 23 December 2004].

29 IFLA/IPA press release October 2001. www.ifla.org/V/press/ ifla-ipa.htm [accessed 23 December 2004].

30 IFLA, *Limitations and Exceptions to Copyright and Neighbouring Rights in the Digital Environment: an international library perspective*, www.ifla.org/III/clm/p1/ilp.htm [accessed 23 December 2004].

31 www.un.org/Overview/rights.html [accessed 23 December 2004].

32 May, C. *Digital Rights Management and the Breakdown of Social Norms*, www.firstmonday.org/issues/issue8_11/may/ [accessed 27 November 2004].

33 *Intellectual Property on the Internet: a survey of issues*, op. cit.

34 *Promoting Innovation and Economic Growth: the special problem of digital intellectual property*, op. cit.

35 *Intellectual Property on the Internet: a survey of issues*, op. cit.

36 EBLIDA position paper on DRMS, www.eblida.org/position/DRMS_Position_Feb03.pdf [accessed 23 December 2004].

37 Publishers Association, *Digital Rights Management: to avoid confusion*, op. cit.

38 CEN (2003) *Digital Rights Management: final report*, http://europa.eu.int/comm/enterprise/ict/policy/doc/drm.pdf [accessed 23 December 2004].

39 European Commission (2004) *The Management of Copyright and Related Rights in the Internal Market*, COM (2004) 261 final.

40 Ibid., section 1.2.5, para. 5.

3 The right to digitize: gaining copyright clearance to create digital collections of text

Helen Pickering

Introduction

This chapter looks at the processes of copyright clearance, required to convert print material into digital, specifically in the context of use by students and staff at higher or further education institutions. It covers the following areas: whether clearance is needed, how to find out who holds the rights, finding the contact details for rights holders, getting the rights holders to grant permission, some common terms and conditions, and finally some issues for the requesting institutions.

This chapter also covers the most common courses of action, and highlights some problems which may occur during the process.

It should be noted that the descriptions of licences in this chapter are not intended as definitive summaries, and when a feature is highlighted to illustrate a particular point it does not necessarily reflect the relative importance of that feature within the licence as a whole.

Is clearance required?

The first question to be asked when you want to create a digital copy is, 'Do I need to get permission for this?' Being able to make this decision may depend on having some knowledge of copyright and how it works. There are several guides to copyright currently in print (see Further Reading at the end of this chapter) and, if there is any doubt, it is always best to err on the side of caution and ask permission.

There are several reasons why permission may not be necessary. They are outlined below.

Materials in the public domain

Work which is in the public domain can be digitized at will and by anyone. No permission is necessary. For material to be in the public domain, both the typographical rights (which relate to the layout and typography of the item) and the copyright relating to the actual content must have expired. Typographical rights last for 25 years from the first publication of an edition. So, after 25 years, typographical rights cannot be used as a reason to prevent the making of a copy, even if the book is still in print using the same typography.

The duration for the copyright relating to the content is more complicated. The general rule is that copyright lasts for the author's life plus 70 years, or, more specifically, 70 years from the end of the year in which the author died (i.e. if the author dies in June 2000, the copyright expires on 31 December 2070). However, if the work is published anonymously, or has no personal author (e.g. company reports), then copyright expires 70 years from the first publication. This 70-year duration assumes that the material was published inside the European Economic Area (EEA).[1] If the material was published outside the EEA, then the duration of copyright is governed by the laws of the country in which it was published. (The duration would normally be at least 50 years from either the death of the author, or from first publication where there is no personal author, because most countries are signatories to the Berne Convention which provides for this minimum level of protection.) There are a couple of exceptions to this rule in the UK, where perpetual copyright has been granted:

- *Peter Pan* – section 301 of the CDPA provides for the Hospital for Sick Children at Great Ormond Street in London to benefit from the royalties in the work by Sir James Matthew Barrie, even though the copyright expired in the work on 31 December 1987.
- the printing of the Authorized (King James) Version of the Bible is covered by royal letters patent which to this day give the Crown prerogative over the copying of the King James Bible.

The duration of Crown Copyright material is either 125 years from the year in which it was created, or 50 years from the date of the first commercial publication – the latter applies only if material is published during the first 75 years after creation.

It should also be remembered that the main author may not be the only one holding copyright – translators have copyright in their translation, a new introduction will be in copyright, and editors may have written accompanying notes or edited a public domain text to the extent that their contribution, or even the text as a whole, is covered by copyright. As an example, while the original works of Plato are in the public domain, it is likely that recent translations and editions are still protected.

Government publications

In the UK, materials written by employees of the Crown are subject to Crown Copyright, and this includes most government publications. Copyright in the following materials has been waived:

- Acts of the UK Parliament and the Northern Ireland Assembly
- Statutory Instruments including those made by the National Assembly for Wales
- Statutory Rules of Northern Ireland
- Explanatory Notes to the above Acts.

This waiver is subject to certain conditions which are listed in paragraph 12 of HMSO Guidance Note 6.[2] (Basically, the reproduction must be accurate, from an official source, up to date, and correctly credited.) Therefore, if the material is covered by the copyright waiver then it can be reproduced without any further permission being required.

In the USA, government publications (including publications by government employees written in the course of their work) are held to be in the public domain.

Copying is covered by an existing licence or by the publisher's policy

If the permission which you require is covered by an existing licence then there is no point in spending time and effort requesting permission again. Several examples of existing licences are described below.

NESLi2 is the UK's national initiative for the licensing of electronic journals on behalf of the higher and further education and research communities (2003–2006). It is a product of the JISC and is underwritten by the Higher Education Funding Council for England on behalf of the funding bodies.

NESli2 follows the three year pilot licence (1995–1997) and the original NESLi (1998–2001) which introduced the concept of a managing agent and piloted the use of a model licence for use in negotiating agreements with publishers. Most recently NESli2 takes over from the JISC Journals Activity. Clause 3.3.1 from the model licence allows articles from the journals to be placed online:

> 3.3 Only Authorised Users may, subject to Clause 4 below:
> 3.3.1 Incorporate parts of the Licensed Material in printed or electronic Course or Study Packs for the use of Authorised Users in the course of instruction . . .[3]

The vast majority of publishers include this clause in their version of the licence, but individual licences should obviously be checked. Blackwell Publishing is an example of a publisher which uses the NESLi2 licence, and makes its site licence available online.[4]

Apart from the NESLi2 licence, many journal publishers give permission for their content to be included in digital course packs as part of the subscription. This grant may appear in the journal (for example, on the copyright page), or it may be explicitly stated in the subscription agreement. Emerald is one example of this; its policy is clearly stated on its web pages:

> Subscribing organizations therefore do NOT need to ask permission and are FREE to:
>
> • make up to 25 copies of a single article for course notes/training purposes etc as long as they are not for re-sale (Requests for larger numbers of photocopies will not be unreasonably withheld on request or necessarily charged for)
> • include photocopies or digital copies of the full text of articles from Emerald journals they subscribe to in their short loan collection or on electronic reading lists [continued on next page]

[continued]
- host articles from subscribed to journals on password protected 'essential reading' intranet/extranet sites for both internal students and registered distance learners.[5]

An example of a smaller publisher making its materials more freely available to subscribers is the American Association for the Advancement of Slavic Studies, Inc. Its website states:

Copying is permitted in accordance with the fair use guidelines of the US Copyright Act of 1976. The association permits the following additional educational uses without permission or payment of fees: academic libraries may place materials from *Slavic Review* on reserve (in multiple photocopied or electronically retrievable form) for students enrolled in specific courses; teachers may reproduce or have reproduced multiple copies (in photocopied or electronic form) for students in their courses.[6]

HMSO has two 'click-use' licences, one of which enables copying of 'core materials' without further permission being necessary. Core material can be defined as meeting the following criteria:[7]

- It is essential to the business of government.
- It explains government policy.
- It is the only source of the information.
- It sets out how the law, in both the UK and EU, must be complied with.
- The citizen will consider the information to be key to their relationship with government.
- There may be a statutory requirement to produce or issue such information.

If your institution has taken out the Core Licence then these materials may be reproduced for free, subject to the terms of the licence.[8] If there is any doubt as to whether the material is 'core' then HMSO's copyright office can be contacted by telephoning 01603 621000 or by e-mailing hmsolicensing@cabinet-office.x.gsi.gov.uk for clarification and, if necessary, permission.

Third-party licences may also allow digitization without the need for further permission. In the UK, the Copyright Licensing Agency[9] is running a trial licence for the further education sector[10] which allows scanning of books and journals published in the UK, within certain extent limits. Its Higher Education licence is expected to follow suit in 2005. Obviously, these licences are available only to the relevant sectors and they have specific limitations in terms of extent and coverage. (See later in this chapter for more detail about the CLA licences.)

Author is lecturer

In most cases a lecturer may digitize material which they have had published without needing permission – provided the material is being used to support their teaching. However, despite moves towards limiting the rights which academic authors grant to their publishers, this is not guaranteed, and the contract with the publisher should be checked. It may even be wise to check with the publisher anyway, the first time the material is used, since many authors do not realize the difference between owning the copyright and owning the right to make further copies. In any event, most publishers are happy to waive, or at least reduce permission fees, where the copy is being used to support the author's teaching.

Fair dealing

The concept of fair dealing has been covered in Chapter 1 of this book, and it cannot be applied to making a digital copy for use by a group of students. It may be used by students making copies for themselves, or by a librarian making a copy for an individual student,[11] but it remains a defence rather than a right and should not be used to create digital copies for systematic use by students or staff.

Clearance routes

Assuming that permission is needed, there are several ways to get permission.

Copyright Licensing Agency (CLA)

The CLA is the UK's reproduction rights organization. It is responsible for licensing the copying of book and journal materials in the UK. At the time of writing it has several digitization licences available to educational institutions; all are under review. The higher education sector currently has a transactional licence allowing scanning and conversion to PDF text, and this requires permission to be sought and granted for each extract used. The further education sector has a trial licence which allows blanket scanning and photocopying, but scans must be an image of the page and cannot be converted to text. Both licences have limits on the amount of material which can be requested. Currently, the CLA's digitization licences cover only UK-based publishers, but is not comprehensive. Expansion to include foreign publishers is not expected in the immediate/near future; and when it does happen, it is likely to be a case of material being added for one country at a time. Those publishers who have authorized the CLA to deal with their clearances may be less willing to deal directly with requests which the CLA could have processed. Additional benefits of the CLA are that requests sent to them are usually processed faster than those sent to rights holders directly, and that their terms of use are consistent across all publishers.

Copyright Clearance Center (CCC)

The CCC is the American equivalent of the CLA. Before being able to request permissions through the CCC, you need to open an account. Once this is open, the licence which allows you to create electronic course packs is the Electronic Course Content Service (ECCS). This, subject to the mandate the CCC has from the rights holder, allows copyright materials to be used in electronic format in course packs and also electronic reserve (i.e. either for use by a specific course, or for general university use.) The CCC has a Digital Permission Service (DPS) which grants permission to fax documents or place them on the internet, an intranet or extranet, but this is aimed at corporate usage. It covers most American publishers and some UK ones. As with the CLA, some US publishers who have authorized the CCC to act on their behalf will not deal with direct requests. The CCC also has the benefit of an online 'quick price' function for checking prices before ordering.

Newspaper Licensing Agency (NLA)

The NLA's educational licence (for students with an admission age over 16 years) has two levels of cover for digital copies, depending on the number of copies expected to be made. Neither of these licences is suitable for storing digital copies of newspaper articles in online course packs, since copies have to be deleted after seven days. Therefore, if you want to use extracts from newspapers, you must contact the newspaper directly to find out if it holds the rights.

Rights holder (publisher/author)

The rights holder is the ultimate source of all permissions, and most will grant permission for their materials to be used in online course packs. Sometimes you will get better terms going directly to the rights holder than using a third party but, equally, some will redirect you to a third party, which adds to the time it takes to actually get the permission.

Agency

If the rights holder is the author, you may be referred to an agency for permission. The agent will negotiate on behalf of the author, or work to its own in-house policies. So it is sometimes possible, and even worthwhile, to try to contact the author directly if the agency does not provide a suitable permission.

HERON

HERON[12] is based in the UK. It offers a copyright clearance and digitization service to subscribing institutions. HERON's coverage of publishers is international and average clearance rates are 90% of all requests for text-based materials (including embedded illustrations). HERON's subscribers are mainly UK universities and colleges who do not have the time, resources or expertise to do copyright clearance and digitization themselves. Clearances are negotiated with a variety of sources, including those listed above, and costs are passed on by HERON from the rights holder to the requesting subscriber for approval before a digital file is created and supplied.

Who holds the rights (and what if I can't find out)?

When trying to identify who actually hold the rights, the first port of call is generally the current or most recent publisher. If it does not hold the rights, it can generally direct you to whomever it thinks holds the rights. A referral is usually due to the rights having been sold to another publisher (for example, Continuum has sold a lot of its business books to Thomson Learning); or it bought/licensed the rights from another publisher, but only for paper copies (this is the case for most anthologies); or the rights have simply reverted to the author.

Occasionally, publishers will not be able to confirm if they hold the rights (contracts get mislaid, especially when publishers merge and sell lists on to other publishers). In this case, the publisher will usually reply with a stock phrase, such as: 'While we have no objection to your proposed use, we cannot grant permission.' At this point it is definitely worth trying to trace the author, who is likely to know who holds the rights now.

There is also a legal complication with older books as to whether the publisher actually has the right to grant permission to digitize. In the 1960s, the concept of digitization did not exist, and was therefore not included in contracts between authors and publishers. So it has been successfully argued in some courts that the publisher cannot hold the rights. (Random House took Rosetta Books to court in the USA because Rosetta published e-book versions of titles which were originally published by Random House in the 1960s. The court found in favour of Rosetta – Random House Inc vs Rosetta Books LLC, 283 F. 3d 490 (2nd Cir., 2002.) However, as long as the publisher's permission grant warrants that it holds the rights, and indemnifies you against any actions resulting from its permission grant, it is safe to assume that you can use the permission from the publisher.

If you have tried all avenues to trace the publisher and the author, and failed, then the decision to digitize the material comes down to a risk assessment. If you decide to create a copy, then it should include a statement to the effect that 'every effort has been made to trace the copyright owner of this material, and anyone claiming copyright should get in touch with xxx'. You should also keep copies of documentation relating to the clearance (or not) of that material, so that you can prove that you did your best to trace the rights holder, and that you have been trying to act in good faith, in case of claims.

How do I locate the rights holder (and what if I can't)?

Once you know who the rights holder is, various sources can be used to obtain contact details. Case Studies 1 and 2 give examples of two such processes. The most obvious source, these days, is the internet. Most publishers have web pages, and can be found from online references. There are also various directories of publishers in print form and online (e.g. *Ulrich's Periodicals Directory* is an invaluable source for tracing current journal publishers; *Babash's Directory of UK Publishers*[13] is fairly comprehensive, although it does not claim to be authoritative; the catalogue of the Association of American University Presses[14] can be a quick way of tracing university presses in the USA). Publishers' contact details can also be found in Bowker's *Books in Print* databases. In addition, trade associations such as the Publishers Association,[15] the Publishers Licensing Society,[16] and the Welsh Books Council[17] can all help to provide contact details for publishers.

If you still can't trace the publisher after searching for its name on the internet and in publisher directories, or only have access to the internet and no other tools, then it is worth checking the bibliographic details (unless you have access to the actual book or journal you want permission to reproduce). Searching for the title on COPAC[18] can provide catalogue records which bring more information about the location of the publisher, and sometimes the whole address. It can also alert you to changes in the publisher. Similarly, searching for the title or ISBN/ISSN on the internet can bring up citations which can help to trace the publishers. If you are on good terms with other publishers' permission departments, they may be willing to provide you with contact details for other publishers as well.

Case study 1: 1950s journal article

Step 1: Request permission from CLA. Referred to publisher.

Step 2: Contact the publisher to see if it holds the rights. The title is no longer published; it does not hold the rights and it has no contact details for the author.

Step 3: Internet search for the author. Author died in 1963; there are no references to other publications. She is mentioned with reference to an exhibition of a collection at a Chicago Museum in 1950.

Step 4: Internet search for the collection. The collection is currently listed at a museum in Germany.

Step 5: Contact museum and ask if it has any contact details for the estate of the author.

Step 6: Reply from the museum stating that it believes there are some distant relations in South Africa, but the last time any contact was made they did not assert any rights. The museum recommends going ahead without seeking their permission.

Case Study 2: 1965 chapter from a collection of essays

Step 1: Request permission from CLA. Referred to publisher.

Step 2: Request permission from publisher. It has no contractual evidence that it holds the rights, and no contact details for the author or editor.

Step 3: Internet search for the author. No obvious contact details available.

Step 4: Internet search for the editor. He died in 1978.

Step 5: Revisit search for author. He is referred to as Emeritus Professor of Statistics at one university and a member of a committee at another university.

Step 5: Contact the first university. It has no record of him in the department.

Step 6: Internet search for committee. Contact the secretary of the committee.

Step 7: Contact the Society of Authors and ALCS. Neither has any records for the author.

Step 8: Reply from the committee's secretary with contact details for the author.

Step 9: Contact the author. Permission granted.

If you are looking for an author rather than a publisher, it can be harder (assuming that the publisher has not passed on your request to the author, or even passed you the author's contact details). As before, one of the best resources is the internet: combining the author's name and words from the title of the book can help to narrow the search and omit other people with the same name. Academic authors who are, or have been, lecturers at universities are generally easier to find than non-academic authors, simply because university web pages are usually very well indexed. Other routes for tracing authors include WATCH (http://tyler.hrc.utexas.edu/), the Society of Authors (www.societyofauthors.net/) and ALCS (www.alcs.co.uk). Another useful route for finding an author's details is to contact a publisher who has worked with them recently, and ask it to pass a letter on for you; or to contact their co-authors to see if they have current contact details.

Obtaining permission: how to ask for permission

In order for permission to be granted, you generally need to provide the following information:

- author and title of the extract you want to reproduce
- author and title of the publication in which the extract appears
- page range
- date of publication (plus volume and issue numbers for journals)
- ISBN/ISSN
- publisher's name (this is for your own information as much as anything)
- number of copies to be made (i.e. number of students on the course, if required for a course)
- course title
- course dates
- your institution.

It can also help if you include:

- format of the copies (e.g. PDF)
- levels of protection available (e.g. individual passwords are needed to be able to access the file)

- whether you subscribe to the journal or hold copies of the book being requested
- whether the lecturer requesting use of the material is also the author
- your reference for the request: if you are requesting a lot of extracts then it is useful to give each one a reference which the publishers quote back at you. Waiting weeks for a reply, which turns out to be a one-line e-mail from a different contact address, and simply says 'Permission Granted' with no indication of which request is being replied to is very frustrating!

Methods of contact

Once you have this information, you should contact whomever you are using to obtain the clearance, and follow their instructions. Many publishers have permissions information on their web pages. If their web pages tell you to fill in a web form, or to contact the CLA or CCC, then you should do that – unless the form or the CLA/CCC does not allow the use which you are requesting. For example, some permissions web forms seem to be tailored to producing physical course packs, and request information about the print run and publication date. These can usually be filled in with a little common sense, but some are simply not suitable. If you choose not to follow the publisher's instructions, then you should explain this in a covering letter with your permission request, or even phone the publisher first. Otherwise you risk receiving a standard reply telling you to follow the instructions on its web pages.

- The CLA provides an e-mail address for licensees who want permission to digitize: clarcs@cla.co.uk. For further information, see www.cla.co.uk/clarcs/index.html.
- The CCC has a web form for orders. It also allows the price to be checked before you place an order. See www.copyright.com.

All publishers accept requests by letter or fax. Most, but by no means all, accept a request by e-mail (though not all accept attachments, so you may need to put the request in the body of the e-mail). Few accept requests by phone, but since the telephone does not provide any hard evidence of either the request or the grant it is best avoided. As already stated, some publishers also have a web form facility for permission requests.

Terms and conditions

Obviously, different rights holders have their own licences with their own terms and conditions. However, the basic terms and conditions usually required for a digital permission grant are as follows:

- Files must be stored and accessed within a secure network (i.e. password protected).
- Access must be restricted to authorized users (either specific to a course or an institution).
- A notice identifying the copyright holder and indicating that the copy is being made by permission must be given.
- Files must be deleted once they are no longer required for the licensed purpose.
- The text of the material must not be edited and must maintain the look and feel of the original.

Variations on these terms include specifying the exact wording which must be used for the copyright notice and setting technical standards for the digitization process.

There are four main licensing models in use within the UK education sector at the moment.

CLA's higher education institution (HEI) digitization licence

The CLA's HEI digitization licence is transactional, and grants permission under two usage models, both of which include illustrations and third-party materials (the publishers specify which model applies):

- The 'Textbook' model grants permission for material to be digitized and converted to text (subject to standards), for use by a specific group of students on an identifiable course/module. The resulting file can be recommended only to those students on the licensed course, although other students at the institution may access the file as long as they find it through their own private research and study. In effect, this maintains the possibility of fair dealing in the electronic environment. This model is commonly known as an 'Electronic Coursepack' in the USA.

- The 'Flat Fee' model allows the same file to be created, but enables any students in the requesting institution to be directed towards it. The default duration of this model is five years. This model is equivalent to the concept of the 'Electronic Reserve' in the USA.

CLA's further education (FE) licence

The CLA's FE licence currently allows digital files to be created without the need for further permission, but the files cannot be converted into text, and remain as images unless the material is physically rekeyed. In addition, the digitization must be done by staff at the further education institution (FEI).

Free permission for subscribers

Some journal publishers are willing to grant free permissions where the requesting institution holds a subscription. For example, Blackwell Publishing's site licence has already been mentioned as allowing journal articles to be included in online course packs without further permission being required; Elsevier currently grants free permission where an active subscription is held – although, as is the case with most publishers, you need to request permission. It is always worth checking the terms of the licences and the information printed in the journal itself in case permission is not needed.

Material to be used when teaching

Another situation where permission fees may be waived, or at least reduced, is where the author wants to use the material to support courses they are teaching. This should be covered in the author's contract, but the publisher will also be able to check its copy of the contract.

Most publisher licences will more or less follow the basic terms and conditions described above. One important difference between the publisher's clearance and an equivalent one from the CLA is that the permission will usually explicitly exclude any copyrighted material from other sources which is incorporated into the selection. It is also likely to specify the credit line which should be included as part of the digital file.

Timescales

The time taken to get permission from rights holders can vary greatly. Factors include:

- **Clearance route taken** – using the CLA or the CCC is usually the fastest route; publishers can reply on the same day, but are more likely to take at least a month; authors are generally fairly quick to reply. Where HERON has a direct licence with a publisher, permissions are granted instantly.
- **Time of year** – permissions departments are always busy from July to October, dealing with requests for the new academic year, therefore requests made during this period are always likely to be delayed. Also, holidays such as Christmas and Easter in the UK, and Thanksgiving in the USA can cause delays and backlogs.
- **The efficiency of the rights holder's permission departments** – if a permissions department is insufficiently staffed, then delays are unavoidable.
- **Publisher size has little effect on the time taken to grant permissions** – some larger ones staff their permission departments to keep clearance time to a minimum, while others retain minimal staff who are expected to deal with constant backlogs.

In Case Study 2 (page 61), it took a week for the CLA to reply to the initial request. The request was then sent to the publisher, who, despite being chased for a reply, took three-and-a-half months to respond that it did not have the contractual details to enable it to grant permission. The committee on which the author sat replied with his contact details on the same day it was contacted, and a letter was sent to the author. The author took another two months to reply with permission. This brings the total time taken to five-and-a-half months (which includes the Christmas holidays).

This is a problematic example and, by comparison, the average time taken to get a response from a publisher through HERON is 29 days (40% of requests take longer). Web pages may give you an indication of the time it is likely to take: Elsevier's permissions departments aim to reply within two weeks, while Random House in the USA states that it will take three to five weeks to reply. However, this is only an indication and, although permissions may be processed faster, it is more likely to take longer, especially at peak times.

Third-party materials

Many books and journals contain material embedded into the main body of text which is subject to third-party permissions. For example, Publisher A has to get permission from Publisher B to include its illustrations in a new book and, as such, Publisher A cannot grant permission to digitize the illustrations as they appear in its book, because it only has the right to include the illustration in its book, and not to license it for further use.

Most permission letters from publishers specifically exclude such materials, and unless the letter warrants that the publisher holds all rights to the material it is granting permission for, it should be assumed that anything credited to another source will need separate clearance. By contrast, the CLA clearances allow all material to be included (by virtue of the fact that it already represents most publishers, and also has an arrangement with the Design and Artists Copyright Society (DACS) enabling illustrations to be included).

Obtaining permission for third-party material is for the most part identical to the process of obtaining permission for the main body of work. The two differences are that:

- It may be harder to trace the rights holder – particularly for an illustration whose credits can be hard to find if you do not have access to the entire book. (A reference of 'Smith, Washington University, 1979' is of no use without access to the references or bibliography.)

- Rights holders are likely to want to see a copy of illustrations which are being requested.

Issues for requesting institutions

Apart from the obvious issues for requesting institutions, such as how they will satisfy the requirements of the permission terms and conditions (especially the technical ones), and how they will educate lecturers and manage expectations, the main issue associated with obtaining permissions is the need for a system to manage the process.

If you are dealing only with a small number of permission requests, then a paper-based system will be sufficient. For example, a table listing the bibliographic details, when the request was sent, when the response was received, what the response was, and any notes, such as chasing of the request. Grouping the requests by rights holder is more efficient because it allows you to deal with all their requests in one go (rather than contacting them separately for each individual request). However, as soon as you have more than one course involved, then either you need to include a reference to which course is involved against each extract, or you must have a separate table for each course – at which point requests for materials by the same publisher get split up. See Figure 3.1.

If you are dealing with more than one course, or even one large course, it is worth considering an electronic management system – even as an Excel spreadsheet (which can also be used as the basis for a mail merge to create the permission request letters). For more complex management systems, databases such as Access and Filemaker can be used to create a bespoke system, or an off-the-shelf solution such as PackTracker[19] (available from HERON) can be used.

Whatever method is used, having a well planned process which can be used for monitoring current permissions and checking past events is essential – both to make the process easier and to give you a past record of what has been done, in case of any queries.

In addition, all licences are subject to terms and conditions, so a good management system is required to keep track of what each licence allows you to do. This may or may not be combined with the system which tracks the process of the clearances.

Course: Demo Study Pack SCB241, 1/9/2004 – 31/8/2005. 25 students				
Biblio	Request sent	Response	Response date	Notes
Basic Publications				
Singh, M., Chapter 1. In: Introduction to Sociology, pp. 51–73. Basic Publications, 2000. 1844389864 [ref 101]	31/3/2004	yes	6/7/2004	30/4/2004 – chased 15/5/2004 – re-sent 16/6/2004 – chased 6/7/2004 – granted at 8p/page/student
Jones, Peter, Cultureshock, pp. 170–175. Basic Publications, 1998. 1844384626 [ref 102]	12/4/2004	yes	6/7/2004	15/5/2004 – chased 16/6/2004 – chased 6/7/2004 granted at 8p/page/student
Society of Social Studies				
Norton, W., Towards an Adequate Exploration of Sociology. In: Journal of Social Views, Vol. 7 (3), pp. 141–143. Society of Social Studies, 1993. 1387–4385 [ref 103]	6/5/2004			6/6/2004 – chased (permission staff on holiday for 2 weeks) 25/6/2004 – chased

Figure 3.1   Example of a basic paper-based permission management system

Summary

To distil the process down to its most basic elements, the steps are:

1   Check whether you need permission.
2   Track down and contact the rights holder.

The permissions process is summarized in Figure 3.2 overleaf.

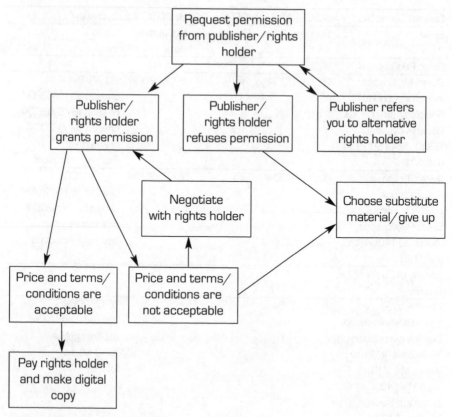

Figure 3.2 The permissions process

Notes and references

1 The EEA is made up of the EU member states, plus Norway, Iceland and Liechtenstein.

2 HMSO, www.hmso.gov.uk/copyright/guidance/gn_06.htm [accessed 23 December 2004].

3 NESLI Licence, clause 3.3.1, www.nesli2.ac.uk/nesli2_lic_010903.htm [accessed 23 December 2004].

4 Blackwell Publishing Site Licence Agreement, clause 3.3, www.blackwellpublishing.com/license/license.pdf [accessed 23 December 2004].

5 Emerald, www.emeraldinsight.com/rpsv/permissions [accessed 23 December 2004].

6   *Slavic Review*, www.econ.uiuc.edu/~slavrev/frames.html [accessed 23 December 2004].
7   HMSO Core Licence, www.hmso.gov.uk/copyright/licences/core/core_licence.htm [accessed 23 December 2004].
8   HMSO Core Licence terms, www.hmso.gov.uk/copyright/licences/core/c_terms.htm [accessed 23 December 2004].
9   CLA, www.cla.co.uk [accessed 23 December 2004].
10 CLA, *FE Licence User Guidelines*, www.cla.co.uk/support/fe/FE-UG-10-03.pdf [accessed 23 December 2004].
11 Joint Information Systems Committee and the Publishers Association (1998) *Guidelines for Fair Dealing in an Electronic Environment*, www.ukoln.ac.uk/services/elib/papers/pa/fair/intro.html [accessed 23 December 2004].
12 HERON, www.heron.ingenta.com [accessed 23 December 2004].
13 *Babash's Directory of UK Publishers*, www.babash.com/Publisher_Index/alphabetic_Index.htm [accessed 23 December 2004].
14 Association of American University Presses, http://aaup.uchicago.edu/ [accessed 23 December 2004].
15 Publishers Association, www.publishers.org.uk/ [accessed 23 December 2004].
16 Publishers Licensing Society, www.pls.org.uk/ [accessed 23 December 2004].
17 Welsh Books Council, www.cllc.org.uk [accessed 23 December 2004].
18 COPAC, www.copac.ac.uk [accessed 23 December 2004].
19 PackTracker, www.heron.ingenta.com/about_packtracker.html [accessed 23 December 2004].

Further reading

Cornish, G. (2004) *Copyright: interpreting the law for libraries, archives and information services*, 4th edn, London, Facet Publishing.
Norman, S. (2004) *Practical Copyright for Information Professionals: the CILIP handbook*, London, Facet Publishing.

4 The right to teach

Linda Purdy

Introduction

This chapter contextualizes the right to teach in relation to digital rights management by exploring the changes in teaching and learning which have affected the sector since the late 1990s. The student body is becoming increasingly diversified with more students entering university from non-traditional backgrounds, and it can no longer be assumed that students will attend the physical campus to engage in the learning process. There is a transition from the physical learning environment to the virtual learning environment in which institutions are required to provide flexible learning, which can be accessed from anywhere and anytime. Higher service demands are placed on universities as students are contributing more in financial terms to their own education. Institutions themselves are under financial pressure as direct government funding per student head has shrunk. In this climate of financial constraints, universities are required to provide learning for a student body with diverse needs, and at the same time maintain quality and standards.

One of the challenges for tutors is to provide relevant resources which will motivate and engage the students, to stimulate creative thought and enhance the learning process. Although many materials, in a variety of formats, are available for purchase they are often not quite what the tutor requires in terms of content match with the curriculum, style of delivery and degree of interactivity. Increasingly, tutors are looking to the development of new materials, which has become a more achievable option owing to the technological developments of recent years. The creation of new resources may involve accessing, adapting or copying third-party materials. Tutors may work as a single author, or with colleagues, or even across institutions on collaborative projects. All of these elements touch on issues associated with copyright in terms of how materials can be used and who owns rights in the materials created.

Recent years have witnessed a change of focus in the teaching and learning process, from a traditional lecture- and seminar-style to a more student-centred approach. Students now play a more active role in their learning; they are increasingly engaged in working with and creating materials which are presented in a digital format. Creation of their own materials and drawing on third-party materials raises digital rights management issues which students are often unaware of.

This chapter outlines copyright issues from the perspectives of both the tutor and student and then explores some of the channels for communicating with the academic community, tutors and students, to raise awareness of the digital rights management issues which are increasingly an integral part of the teaching and learning environment.

Changes in teaching and learning
Nature of the student body

Higher Education in the Learning Society, the report of the National Committee of Inquiry into Higher Education (Dearing, 1997) laid the foundation stones for the Labour government's policies in higher education:

> The purpose of education is life-enhancing: it contributes to the whole quality of life. This recognition of the purpose of higher education in the development of our people, our society, and our economy is central to our vision. In the next century, the economically successful nations will be those which become learning societies: where all are committed, through effective education and training, to lifelong learning.
>
> Dearing, 1997, 1.1, page 7

A central theme in the recommendations of the Dearing Report is the development of a learning society in which higher education plays a pivotal role. The concept of lifelong learning was taken forward in the Green Paper, *The Learning Age* (1998) in which the government

outlined the strategy for making learning more accessible, and for encouraging people to embrace learning and the opportunities that education has to offer, throughout their lives. It set a target of providing an additional 500,000 places on higher education courses by 2002. The government has since extended this target. The 2010 target is for half of all 18 year olds to start a higher education course for the first time by the age of 30; at present 41% of people between the ages 18 and 30 enter higher education for the first time.

As well as increasing the number of people participating in higher education, the government wants to widen participation to ensure that a significant proportion of the additional students entering education come from the lower socio-economic groups. Currently less than 20% of the sons and daughters from part-skilled and unskilled backgrounds enter higher education compared with at least 75% of those from professional families.

The government has also set a target of recruiting an additional 50,000 overseas higher education students by 2005.

The nature of the student body is changing. The educational experiences and educational backgrounds of entrants to higher education will be very different, and this has a significant impact on the content of courses and the way in which students are taught.

Financial investment

Another significant factor in the changing education marketplace is the shift in the cost of higher education away from the tax payers onto the students and the institutions. Some students may opt to study on a part-time course, combining this with a job and perhaps even family commitments. Some students may study by distance learning and never attend the physical university campus. Even the pattern of study for full-time students based on campus is no longer full time in the traditional understanding of that mode of study. The majority of students have to combine studying with part-time work to avoid carrying unmanageable debts with them when they migrate from being undergraduates into newly fledged professionals. These pressures affect not only the amount of time they have available to study, but when and where they study. Today's students need to be able to study at a time and place convenient to them, to dovetail their study with the other demands in their lives.

Students are now making a higher personal financial investment in their education and, consequently, have higher expectations of their educational experience. They are making higher service demands on universities at a time when funding per student head has fallen. Dearing noted the 40% drop in funding between 1976 and 1997, and at the present time there is no sign of sector funding increasing to support increased student numbers. Universities UK (UUK) has estimated £10 billion will be needed to meet government expansion targets. The government has made it clear in the Higher Education Bill that Universities should not look to centralized sources for extra revenue, but should look to raising fees and generating income from the student population.

Technology

Dearing highlighted the importance of the role of information technology in meeting the demands faced by the sector:

> We believe that the innovative exploitation of Communications and Information Technology (C&IT) holds out much promise for improving the quality, flexibility and effectiveness of higher education.
>
> Dearing, 1997, 13.1, page 202

> We believe that, for the majority of students, over the next ten years the delivery of some course materials . . . will be conducted by computer.
>
> Dearing, 1997, 13.3, page 202

The predictions of Dearing have been realized. Recent years have seen an explosion in the range of software available for supporting online learning and the virtual learning environment (VLE) has emerged. The VLE provides the facilities that are needed to enable learning to take place in 'virtual space' irrespective of student location or time. VLEs are successfully being blended with traditional approaches to teaching and learning to provide an environment which meets the needs of the changing client group. The optimum environment delivers resources and at the same time preserves the need for social interaction and shared learning. Research at Sheffield Hallam

University (Oyston, 2003, page 192) found that blended learning, encompassing a more varied set of learning experiences, generated a new level of enthusiasm among students which in turn led to increased attendance levels at seminars. The shift in focus from physical classroom to virtual learning environment has considerable resource implications, one of which is the need to provide stimulating learning materials to excite and engage the students.

Tutor's perspective

The Dearing Report acknowledged the need for tutors and students to have access to, and freedom to use, resources in a digital environment. The report further identified the obstacle created by copyright legislation:

> We have also noted that current copyright legislation (the Copyright, Designs and Patents Act 1988) precludes the use by individuals of copyright digital information without clearance by the copyright owner, which may take weeks. These delays hamper the speed of interaction between student and teacher and make unnecessary demands on staff time . . . . We recommend to the Government that it should review existing copyright legislation and consider how it might be amended to facilitate greater ease of use of copyright materials in digital form by teachers and researchers.
>
> Dearing Report, 1997, 13.34, Recommendation 43, page 209

This recommendation was made in 1997. Six years later new copyright legislation was introduced in the form of the Copyright and Related Rights Regulations 2003 (SI 2003 2498); the UK implementation of the European Directive (2001/29/EC). Very disappointingly Dearing's recommendation was not evident in the new legislation; conversely the government (albeit owing to European direction) has made it easier for rights holders to restrict the use of digital resources. Pressure for tighter controls came from the music industry and large software houses, and, despite extensive lobbying from the education and information sector, the net result was a shifting in balance from the rights of individuals towards copyright holders. The Statutory Instrument places greater emphasis on the use of technological protection measures, and it is illegal to remove or modify them without the permission of the copyright holder. An application may be made to the Secretary of State to require the removal of protection measures which prevent individuals benefiting from the copyright exceptions granted by statute. In reality this is a token gesture. The bureaucratic process is likely to deter users from following this course of action, and the timescales involved are likely to far exceed the moment of need.

This section addresses the issues facing a tutor in developing exciting and stimulating digital resources for access by students on and off campus. In developing teaching materials a tutor will wish to draw upon the abundance of intellectual property already created for the benefit of society.

When searching for resources and selecting materials to use, tutors need to be cognizant of the following categories that materials, and permissible usage of those materials, may fall into:

They may be:

- out of copyright protection
- copyright free
- protected by copyright legislation with use permitted under 'exceptions'
- covered by the terms and conditions of a licensing agreement.

Use of materials over and above any of these may be made only with the permission of the rights holder, and applying for permission can be a time-consuming and lengthy process. It can be difficult to identify and track down the rights holder; having tracked them down they may be slow to respond and may of course charge a fee. (See Chapter 3.) Tutors are frequently working to tight deadlines; they may not have the luxury of planning and preparing course materials months ahead of time. Also, money for paying rights holders' fees is very limited.

The considerations identified above are examined in relation to a range of media and their use within an e-learning environment.

Moving images and sound

A large amount of material is available from a range of sources, with

terms and conditions of use varying according to statute, licensing terms or limitations stipulated by rights holders.

Off-air recording of broadcast materials

Section 35 of the Copyright, Designs and Patents Act 1988, as amended by the Copyright and Related Rights Regulations (SI 2003/2498) gives educational establishments (as defined by Statutory Instrument) the right to record off-air any TV and radio broadcasts without infringing copyright. If a certified licensing scheme is in place, establishments are obliged to subscribe to the scheme. Two schemes are in operation: the Educational Recording Agency (ERA) Licence and the Open University Licence. The former is the most significant in terms of the range of materials available and the flexibility with which they may be used. The ERA Licence covers BBC, ITV, Channel 4 and Channel 5 output which may be recorded, held and used long term for the educational purposes of the licence holder. Satellite broadcasts are not covered by a licensing scheme and may therefore be freely recorded under section 35 of the Act. Programmes delivered via the internet are defined by legislation as broadcasts if they are made available at a time dictated by the broadcaster, and as such may be freely recorded. However, if a programme can be accessed at a time chosen by the user, it is not a broadcast: it constitutes an 'on-demand service' which may not be recorded under section 35. Broadcasts recorded under section 35 must be fully acknowledged and the educational purpose must be non-commercial.

A wealth of material is available from broadcast output but the value to educational institutions is severely restricted by 'the right of communication to the public' clause in SI 2003/2498. Only the copyright owner has the right to make their work available by electronic transmission so that members of the public may access it at a time and from a place convenient to them. This means that broadcast output may be recorded but cannot be made accessible from within the VLE. It has already been identified that the educational environment is changing. Students are spending less time in the physical building and need to access resources from a place and at a time convenient to them. Unless TV output can be made available in this way the wonderfully rich and valuable resources will be under-utilized in education.

The ERA Board is aware of the changes taking place in the education environment and is responding to feedback from the sector. Helen Nicholson (Chief Executive) reported at a recent conference (Learning on Screen, British Universities Film and Video Council and Society for Screen Based Learning, April 2004) that discussions are taking place with rights holders with a view to introducing an ERA Plus Licence to permit inclusion of material recorded under licence into VLEs, or other electronic transmissions, for delivery on and off campus.

Internet resources

A large amount of video material is available on the internet for educational use. One site of particular note is Educational Media OnLine (www.emol.ac.uk) which is the product of a Joint Information Systems Committee (JISC) funded project led by the British Universities Film and Video Council (BUFVC) in partnership with the Open University. It consists of ten video collections with footage covering life sciences, social sciences and history; each video has a detailed catalogue description with footage divided into downloadable segments. Copyright in this material has been cleared for use within further and higher education. Permissible uses are extensive, ranging from using broadcasts within a VLE and inclusion in Powerpoint presentations, to taking screen grabs of individual images for use in print and electronic teaching and learning materials.

It is an exemplary resource available to the tutor and student. The project team has clearly thought about the needs of the educational community and has an understanding of the changes in teaching and learning and the emerging digital educational environment. The level of content detail for each video segment means the user is able to make a decision about how useful the clip will be without having to first download and view the footage; this is a great aid in the selection process. Rights have been cleared to allow users flexibility in how the content is used. There is potential for the tutor to use it in exciting and imaginative ways when developing learning resources, for access by students on and off campus. There is basically no restriction on use of the material so long as it is used for the educational purposes of the institution and the identifying project logo is not removed from the video clip.

Clearing rights

Many more resources are becoming available to the educational community but their value lies in having sufficient rights cleared to enable flexibility of use. Rights holders are very anxious about making their intellectual property available in a digital environment and are fearful of unfair exploitation by the education community. A greater understanding of the relative positions of rights holders and academic users is necessary. Rights holders are probably unaware of the pedagogical and technological changes in teaching and learning; how resources are used; and how they can be protected; and how use can be restricted even when accessed from outside the physical building. For their part, academic users need to respect the property of copyright owners and the moral rights of creators; to fully acknowledge work; and use it in an appropriate manner within legislative and licensing terms.

Clearing rights for moving images and sound could be expensive depending on who the copyright holder is. Professional organizations and institutes are more likely to be receptive to the educational aims of the VLE and be willing to grant permission free of charge on condition that the reproduction is good quality and a full acknowledgement is made. Commercial companies are more likely to levy fees, which could vary from a token amount to sizeable sums. It is important, when clearing rights, to be specific about what is required. For example, will the resource be accessible to students on and off campus? Will the material be available to any member of the educational establishment or limited to a particular cohort of students? Will the e-learning resource be developed as a commercial venture? These are the considerations which are likely to affect the fees charged. The rights holder will also want to know the context in which their material is being used.

Production in-house

In-house generated video is another option, especially now that digital cameras and editing equipment are easy to use. Depending on the nature of the footage, a higher professional standard may be required, and many institutions have internal TV units that can provide this service. Although the rights in the video will belong to the institution, it is important to remember that individuals appearing in the video will have performer's rights and it is necessary to have written permission from them to use the footage. A 'release form' is a simple and easy way of recording permissions. The form should clearly state how the footage may be used; if it is envisaged that the material may be required for another purpose in the future, a statement to this effect should be included in the form. See the sample release form in Figure 4.1.

Still images

Tutors may wish to incorporate still images (photographs or diagrams) in their VLE, either because they are essential to the content or perhaps just to make the site more interesting. It is a common misconception that use for educational purposes is acceptable. Tutors are often unaware of the rights clearance process, the timescales involved and the likelihood of fees being charged. Depending on how essential the image is it may or may not be worthwhile attempting to clear rights. It is always worth considering other options, for example:

- internet resources which are free of charge for educational use, such as British Pathé (www.britishpathe.com), ARKive (www.arkive.org), Visual Arts Data Service (http://vads.ahds.ac.uk/fineart/), Educational Media OnLine (www.emol.ac.uk), etc.
- creating your own, remembering to get a signed 'release form' from individuals included in any photographs (see Figure 4.1).

A frequent query from tutors is whether or not it is permissible to scan a diagram or table from another source and embed it within their own teaching materials. It is often assumed that this is acceptable if an acknowledgement is given. This is not the case: permission must

---

Release Form

Name: _____

Address: _____

_____

I consent and agree that [name of institution], its employees or agents, have the right to interview, photograph or video me [and/or my property] for possible inclusion in [details of the website/package]

I release to [name of institution], its employees or agents, the right to use, at their discretion, the material in print or digital form within the above context for the educational purposes of staff and students at [name of institution].

I agree that the materials may be used for other non commercial purposes at the discretion of [name of institution].

I am at least 18 years of age, have read and understand the above statements and am competent to execute this agreement.

Should commercial exploitation of the materials be considered at a later stage your permission will be sought.

Unless otherwise stated your name and contact details will be kept confidential.

Signed...

Date...

Figure 4.1   Sample release form

be obtained from the copyright holder to scan and reproduce their work; if the item is already in digital form, permission is needed to copy it. Another false assumption is that permission is not required if the item is not copied, but is instead adapted in some way to create a slightly different version. The right of adaptation is a reserved right for the copyright holder and permission must be obtained. Scanning and adapting someone's work might also be construed as breaching the moral rights of the author, that is the right of the author to object to derogatory treatment.

Websites

There is a misconception that material published on the internet is in the public domain and 'freely' available: downloading material from the internet and linking to websites is fairly common practice. It is assumed that because it is free to view it can be freely used, but materials published on the internet are protected by copyright and they cannot be reproduced without permission, unless there is a statement to the contrary. Before seeking permission it is a good idea to check the website: conditions relating to usage of content may be stated here, hidden under such headings as disclaimer, liability, copyright, terms and conditions. In addition, contact details are usually given for requests to reproduce content over and above the permitted limits. While it is common practice to make hypertext links to internet resources it must be remembered that web pages are the intellectual property of another party and certain practices have to be followed. For example, it is good practice to:

- Make text links rather than only stating a URL because this more clearly identifies the copyright holder.
- Open any link in a new browser window. Some VLEs default to framing with the VLE banner, etc. and this could be construed as passing off, misleading the user on the identity of the true owner of the site.
- Gain permission to use logos. This is not only good practice but legally essential because logos may be registered trademarks and it is an offence to reproduce them without the rights holder's permission.

One area of debate is the practice of deep linking. The safest approach is that recommended by the European Commission IPR Helpdesk, which recommends linking to the home pages and seeking permission to deep link. Many sites are happy to give permission, but some may refuse. They may refuse because the home page contains advertising and it is a condition of their contract with advertisers that traffic to the site is directed via the home pages. Other copyright owners refuse permission because their site is constantly changing and they cannot guarantee that content will always be found at a specific address; they have concerns that links may not be kept up to date and this may reflect badly on them. If the decision is taken to go ahead with a deep link without obtaining permission the tutor must be prepared to remove any such link should the rights holder subsequently object.

Text

At the time of writing this chapter a blanket digitization licence does not exist for the higher education community as it does for the further education sector, so a tutor wishing to digitize an article from a journal or pages from a book must seek permission. Several options are available:

- Seek permission from the rights holder.
- Seek permission via the Copyright Licensing Agency (CLA), which has mandates from some rights holders.
- Seek permission via HERON, a copyright clearance service available to further and higher education member institutions. (See Chapter 3 for more information.)

N.B. A UUK-SCOP working group has been negotiating a digitization licence with the CLA which is likely to be introduced during 2005.

Educational exceptions

The Copyright, Designs and Patents Act 1988 makes special provisions for the use of copyright material by the education sector. One of these exceptions, the right to record broadcast material, was considered earlier. There are two other exceptions of particular note when considering uses of materials in the digital environment:

- Section 32(2) makes an exception for film studies courses by making it permissible to copy a sound recording, film (including video) or broadcast for the purpose of giving or receiving instruction in the making of film or film sound tracks, provided the copying is done by the student or tutor, sufficient acknowledgement is made and the instruction is for non-commercial purposes.

- Another exception available to tutors and students is copying under section 32(3): 'Copyright is not infringed by anything done for the purpose of an examination by way of setting the questions, communicating questions to the candidates or answering the questions, provided that the questions are accompanied by a sufficient acknowledgement.' Care should be taken not to seize on this useful exception, which allows educational users a large degree of freedom of use, by extending the principle to copy to use in formative assessment and curriculum materials. Copying under this exception can be done only for closed examinations and summative assessment, that is when the assessment mark counts as part of the student's final mark, and the copy can be used only by the students taking the assessment and the tutor marking the assessment. So, it is not permissible to post students' work, which includes materials copied under this exception, on the intranet for other students to see as exemplars of good work, an activity which tutors would consider to be justifiable educational use of no economic harm to the rights holders.

Who owns rights?

Who owns the rights? This is a frequent question asked by academics about materials they produce, be it an article for publication in an electronic journal or e-learning materials developed for the VLE. The Copyright, Designs and Patents Act 1988, section 11(2) states that where a copyright work has been produced by someone 'in the course of his employment, his employer is the first owner of any copyright in the work subject to any agreement to the contrary'. An important phrase is 'in the course of his employment'. It is not entirely dependent on when or where the materials were created but whether or not they were created as part of the required duties of the employee. This is an area of much debate in academia. A widely adopted practice in institutions is for the tutor to own copyright in articles, conference papers and books, and for the institution to own copyright in teaching materials, including materials produced for the VLE. Where opportunities exist for commercial exploitation of teaching resources, royalties are generally shared between the employer and the employee. This is recognition of the contribution of the employee and is an incentive to staff to generate more resources.

Aligned to the misconception that tutors own the copyright in materials they have produced is the false understanding that tutors may use materials they created while working at University A when they take up a new post at University B. As already stated, copyright in teaching materials belongs to the university and they may be used elsewhere only with the university's permission.

Education is increasingly entering the commercial domain and content has a market value. It is important that institutions have clear copyright ownership and remuneration policies in place to avoid misunderstandings and to encourage tutors to be innovative and develop new resources using materials in imaginative ways. Recommendations for good practice and model contracts can be found in the Higher Education Funding Council for England (HEFCE) report *Intellectual Property Rights in e-learning Programmes*, which explores issues of copyright ownership in e-learning materials. As well as normal contracts of employment, formal agreements will be required to cover work specially commissioned, that is work done outside the terms of the job specification.

Academics are under pressure to publish in refereed journals to improve their institution's rating in the research assessment exercise; a higher rating attracts more funding to the university. It is standard practice for journal publishers to ask contributors to assign rights to the publisher. Increasingly tutors are realizing that this comes at a price. Should a tutor wish to reproduce in the VLE an article of which they are the author, they will have to obtain the permission of the publisher, the copyright owner, and probably have to pay fees for the privilege of using material they have written. To safeguard against this happening, tutors should take the initiative and negotiate a clause in their publishing contract, to allow them to retain rights to use the materials they have created in whatever ways they want for their own teaching purposes.

Consortia and collaborative projects can be a copyright nightmare if copyright ownership is not discussed and agreed at the outset. Key issues to address are:

- Who owns the software?
- Who owns the copyright in the materials produced?

- What is the division of benefits resulting from commercial exploitation?
- What rights do partners have to use and further develop the 'product' within their own institution (that is the right to teach using their own materials)?

At the beginning of a project, partners, in their enthusiasm for developing the 'product', often overlook these issues. However, they will arise at some stage and they can be much harder to resolve at later stages. It is vital that partners sign a formal agreement at the outset; an example of an agreement can be found in Appendix 2 of the Joint Information Systems Committee/Teaching and Learning Technology Programme *Copyright Guidelines for JISC and TLTP Projects* (1998).

In summary, a tutor has access to a wealth of third-party materials to draw upon when creating teaching and learning materials but must tread with caution. Usage of the materials is governed by many different copyright regulations and licensing terms. We are a long way from the utopia recommended by Dearing, which could have been achieved if the government had extended the 'examination exception' to cover educational use in general. This was never likely to happen. DfEE's (1998) response to Dearing Recommendation 43 was to note concern and say the key to securing greater ease of use lay in licensing agreements. We live in the digital age when high-quality copies can be produced and distributed quickly and easily, and rights holders have natural concerns about their economic rights. Commercialism is central to everything. It has increasingly entered the higher education sector, and has manifested itself in the debates on ownership of rights. Ownership of copyright in materials created within institutions is an important issue to be addressed. JISC has recommended that institutions ensure they have policies in place which clarify copyright ownership of the different types of materials created by staff; it further recommends greater co-ordination and consistency between institutions regarding their policies of ownership of intellectual property rights (IPR) and assignment or licensing to commercial publishers to ensure a consistency across the education sector as a whole.

Student's perspective

Digital rights management from a student perspective broadly falls into two areas:

- using third-party materials for research and private study, and producing coursework for assessment
- ownership of rights in materials created during a course of study.

Using third-party materials

The Copyright, Designs and Patents Act 1988 makes some provision for students to copy third-party materials under the defence of 'fair dealing for research and private study for non-commercial purposes'. This defence applies to materials which fall in the category of 'literary, dramatic, musical and artistic works'; and the amount which may be copied, while not stipulated in the legislation, is widely accepted to be:

- one article from a journal issue
- one chapter from a book, or extracts totalling no more than 5%
- 10% from short reports or pamphlets without chapters, provided the total copied is no more than 20 pages.

The Act does not specifically mention electronic formats, but the basic principles detailed in the legislation are applied to categories of materials whether they are presented in a paper, analogue or digital format.

The Joint Information Systems Committee and the Publishers Association (1998) produced a useful set of guidelines which apply the 'fair dealing' concept to digital texts. The guidelines give scenarios of what it would, and would not, be considered fair for a student to do in terms of copying electronic publications. The following are considered reasonable actions for a student engaging in research and private study for non-commercial purposes:

- incidental copying to disk involved in the viewing of part or all of an electronic publication
- printing onto paper one copy of part of an electronic publication, within the accepted limits noted above

- making a permanent electronic copy of part of an electronic publication to refer to later.

These guidelines are helpful at the present time but, as they themselves recognize, publishing practices involving works on digital media will change over time: 'For example, the traditional practice in academic journals produced in print medium, of publishing discrete parts of such journals each year, might well be replaced in the digital medium by publication of material (articles, reviews, etc.) as and when it becomes available.' (JISC and PA, *Guidelines for Fair Dealing in an Electronic Environment*, page 2). This will make it very difficult to determine what constitutes part of a publication, and how much it is fair to copy.

The JISC guidelines identify the complex copyright issues surrounding use of materials other than text and consequently limit advice to publications which are either all text or primarily text. With regard to illustrations, the report emphasizes these may be copied only if they are integral to the text, that is they support the text. It is a completely different scenario if the text supports the images: 'Copying and transmitting an image, or set of images, with little or no text associated with them is probably not fair dealing' (JISC and PA, *Guidelines for Fair Dealing in an Electronic Environment*, page 12). This is very limiting for students who will want to reproduce illustrations and use them in their coursework. They are similarly restricted in that the defence of 'fair dealing for research and private study for non-commercial purposes' does not extend to film, video and audio recordings.

Multimedia is becoming more a part of the educational experience in the same way that it is becoming part of society in general. Students' research is unlikely to be limited to text materials; they will explore the wealth of resources including videos, TV broadcasts, audio recordings and websites, which by their very nature are often 'multimedia'. How frustrating if this material falls outside the scope of what students can use. Education should be an enriching, exciting and stimulating experience, where for legitimate educational purposes a student should be able to draw on the full range of materials. Legislation does go part way to acknowledging this need. Although the 'fair dealing for research and private study for non-commercial purposes' defence is restricted primarily to text the law does make other provisions. A defence which opens up more options to students is 'fair dealing for criticism or review', which applies to copying of all categories of material, provided that acknowledgement is given. But care should be taken. Although the legislation does not define 'criticism and review', it is accepted that under this defence materials should be copied only in the context of a critique, and they should not be used for illustrative purposes.

Another option available to students is copying under section 32(3) of the Copyright, Designs and Patents Act 1988; that is copying for examination or assessment purposes. As already discussed in the previous section 'Tutor's Perspective' this right can be used only for examinations or summative assessment, not for coursework or formative assessment where the marks are not part of the student's final mark. The 'examination right' is a valuable right which enables the student to create more imaginative work drawing on a range of materials in all formats. However, it does have limitations in terms of the wider educational experience and today's teaching and learning environment. Students are part of a learning and sharing culture where exemplary work is made available to guide and inspire other students. The concepts of peer review and online discussion are increasingly part of the educational experience, but sharing and exposing work which includes third-party materials copied under section 32(3) is not permissible.

Ownership of rights

Students are not employees of an institution and copyright in works they produce does not automatically belong to the institution as it does in the case of tutors. In law, an institution has no right to reproduce, publish or use the materials created by students without the permission of the student. Ownership of copyright can be transferred in advance and many institutions are now adopting the practice of requiring students to transfer all intellectual property rights in materials they produce in the course of their studies to the university. This is done from a paternalistic point of view because the university is in a much better position to protect the rights and, should commercial exploitation be an option, to pursue this and share remuneration from royalties with the student. Such agreements are often part of the university regulations which students agree and sign at the time of enrolment. It is questionable if this approach would be upheld by courts because it is likely students are unaware of what they have agreed to. To be legally binding it should be drawn to the student's attention at the time of enrolment and should not be a compulsory clause.

The issue of ownership of copyright becomes more complex in the context of the diverse nature of today's student body. Students who are supported by their employer may be undertaking work-related projects involving confidential information, or they may be a research student funded by a commercial operation. These more complex situations require arrangements to be in place to deal with copyright and IPR ownership.

Communicating with the user

The key piece of copyright legislation, the Copyright, Designs and Patents Act 1988, has been updated by a number of Statutory Instruments making it very difficult to keep track of changes; a reprinting of current legislation amalgamating all of the changes is long overdue. In addition, interpretation of the legislation is hampered by a lack of definition of terms and phrases leading to grey areas which rely on case-law for clarification.

The JISC Senior Management Briefing Paper 5 (1998) acknowledges the complexity of copyright and sets out recommendations to higher education institutions about setting a copyright policy to:

- Educate staff and students about the basics of copyright and acceptable practice
- Protect senior executives and institutions against legal actions arising from infringement of copyright laws.

Digital rights management lies within the framework of copyright and should therefore be included in an institutional copyright policy. Given the growth in digital materials and the increasing use of the digital environment for teaching and learning it is good practice to

make DRM issues explicit in any institutional policy or regulations.
The policy needs to address two aspects of rights management:

* using third-party materials
* ownership of rights.

The JISC recommendations to higher education institutions regarding
copyright policy include the following:

* All staff and students should be educated on what is acceptable
  practice.
* Copyright infringement by students should be a disciplinary
  offence under university regulations.
* Copyright infringement by staff should be a disciplinary offence
  under the terms of the staff contract of employment.
* Downloading material from the internet to incorporate into
  assignments should be covered under both plagiarism and
  copyright regulations.
* Institutions should ensure that copying by staff and students does
  not exceed limits permissible under law and licensing agreements.
* Institutions should review the measures they have in place to
  protect materials they place on the world wide web.
* Institutions should have a clear policy on ownership of rights in
  materials created by staff, and this should be stated in all staff
  employment contracts.
* Institutions should consider the appointment of a copyright
  expert to advise and educate staff and students.
* Institutions should educate staff on the importance of not giving
  away 'all rights' to publishers.
* Institutions need a procedure to expedite clearance on materials
  in which they own the rights.

The JISC recommendations, while extensive, are not all encompassing
and other areas need to be considered and included, for example
ownership of rights in materials created by students. An institutional
policy needs to state where responsibility for infringement lies and
who owns rights in materials created; they should also include a duty
to educate the 'academic community'.

Enforcing copyright compliance is a difficult issue. While JISC recommends that 'institutions should ensure that copying by staff and students does not exceed limits permissible under law and licensing agreements', this is unenforceable in practice. In the event of a court case, the employer would be liable so it is vital they take responsibility for educating staff and students and have procedures in place for dealing with offenders.

Educating the user

Library and information professionals have long acknowledged that they have a role to play in supporting their users in gaining access to, and using, information in all formats, while at the same time respecting the economic rights of authors and creators of materials. It is usually this group of professionals that takes on the role of educating users in the basics of copyright law and providing guidance in interpreting the law, so users understand what the law means in relation to the issues facing them.

It is important to use as many channels of communication as possible and to provide the information in a digestible format. Users are often unaware of the importance of copyright and the significance of their actions. The way in which the information professional communicates this basic understanding to the users can affect the impact of the message. For example, one paper document detailing all of the legislative and licensing terms relevant to the institution would be unlikely to have much impact on staff and students. It would be more effective, and more helpful, to provide the information which is appropriate to the circumstances and needs of the users.

The following are some practical suggestions for how the message can be conveyed:

- A brief leaflet could highlight the importance of copyright and what it means in practical terms for the user; it might have references to sources of more detailed information and guidance.
- Web pages could be aimed at different user groups, addressing issues likely to be of concern to those groups; presenting the information in question-and-answer form makes it more digestible and easier for the user to find the guidance they need.

- Guidance for staff developing resources for use in the VLE might again be presented in a question-and-answer form, perhaps with a flow chart and even a quiz, 'What do you know about copyright?'
- Meeting face to face with users often has more impact. It also gives users an opportunity to air concerns and explore issues specific to their projects. Meetings might be:
  - at an institutional level: for example, presentations at new-staff courses and staff development workshops
  - at a local level: for example, a meeting with a group of tutors, at subject or departmental level, or a project group
  - at an individual level: for example, meeting tutors individually to work through DRM issues of specific concern to them.
- Appropriate notices could be given *in situ* where users may use equipment to copy materials, for example by scanners, in editing suites.

Communicating with the student body is harder than communicating with tutors because it is a larger and more disparate body. Tutors are an important conduit in reaching students. By raising the awareness of tutors and making them more aware of digital rights issues they are able to cascade their knowledge to students when setting assignments and coursework. They in turn have a responsibility to help students understand the legal implications of their actions.

The future

A key issue in the development of the digital teaching and learning environment is access to, and utilization of, third-party materials for the creation of new resources. The development of high-quality learning materials is both time consuming and expensive, thus making it a goal difficult to achieve.

In the 1990s, collaboration between academic institutions was seen to be a way of meeting the need: 'Collaboration between institutions, on the other hand, is more efficient in terms of staff time, allows criterion-referenced selection by an inter-institutional discipline-based review panel, and integrates effort, expertise and experience in a difficult new area' (Laurillard, 1993, page 225). The government made considerable investment in a number of major national projects such as those funded through the UK Teaching and Learning Technology Initiative. Disappointingly the digital products developed under this initiative have not been widely adopted by the academic community. When evaluating suitability of existing materials, tutors often look for an almost exact match with their curriculum; this is rarely found. What is ideal for one tutor, may be, at best, only acceptable by another; there is inevitably a desire to develop a resource that exactly matches the needs of their course and their students.

Within the academic community there is increasing awareness of the value of learning objects, digital materials at varying levels of granularity which can be used by tutors and students when creating their own resources. The value of the learning objects will depend on good metadata to help the user identify suitable materials, and then rights cleared to allow flexible use within a changing educational scene, as identified earlier in this chapter. The government is committed to increasing access to digital resources to support e-learning and via the JISC funds many initiatives and projects have been created. The way forward is the creation of national repositories of reusable copyright-cleared digital resources, which may be used to enable and stimulate creative work by tutors and students.

This ideal is embodied in the Creative Commons initiative which was founded in the USA in 2001 with the goal to 'build a layer of reasonable, flexible copyright in the face of increasingly restrictive default rules' (Creative Commons). The Creative Commons licences are designed to allow creators of websites, music, film, photography, literature and courseware to retain their copyright while licensing their work as free for certain uses. The aim is 'not only to increase the sum of raw source material online, but also to make access to that material cheaper and easier' (Creative Commons). Creators can attach a Creative Commons licence to their work, selecting from four basic conditions: attribution requirement, no commercial use, no derivative works, share alike. There are up to 11 possible combinations for rights holders to tailor a licence to suit their own particular requirements. Materials are freed up for the public good, rights holders retain protection in a way chosen by themselves and the bureaucratic process of clearing rights is minimized.

Summary

This chapter has looked at the changes in teaching and learning, and the development of the digital learning environment. It has considered the DRM issues of tutors and students accessing and using resources created by someone else, and also considered ownership rights in newly created materials. It has addressed the need for institutions to incorporate these DRM issues into their policies and the need for institutions to educate their employees and students. It has concluded by considering how the need for access to third-party reusable resources might be met.

References

Copyright and Related Rights Regulations 2003 (SI 2003/2498).

Copyright Designs and Patents Act 1988.

Creative Commons, *'Some Rights Reserved': building a layer of reasonable copyright*, http://creativecommons.org/learn/aboutus/ [accessed 23 December 2004].

DfEE (1998) *Higher Education for the 21st Century: response to the Dearing Report*, www.lifelonglearning.co.uk/dearing [accessed 23 December 2004].

Higher Education Funding Council for England (2003) *Intellectual Property Rights in e-learning Programmes: good practice guidance for senior managers*, 2003/08, www.hefce.ac.uk/pubs/hefce/2003/03_08.htm [accessed 23 December 2004].

IPR Helpdesk, *Copyright and Internet Guide*, www.ipr-helpdesk.org. Follow links to Intellectual Property, Copyright [accessed 23 December 2004].

Joint Information Systems Committee/Teaching and Learning Technology Programme (1998) *Copyright Guidelines for JISC and TLTP Projects*, eLib Programme Studies C1, JISC.

Joint Information Systems Committee (1998) *Copyright*, Senior Management Briefing Paper 5, JISC.

Joint Information Systems Committee and the Publishers Association (1998) *Guidelines for Fair Dealing in an Electronic Environment*, www.ukoln.ac.uk/services/elib/papers/pa/fair/intro.html [accessed 23 December 2004].

Laurillard, D. (1993) *Rethinking University Teaching: a framework for the effective use of educational technology*, London, Routledge.

National Committee of Inquiry into Higher Education (1997) *Higher Education in the Learning Society* (Dearing Report), London, HMSO.

Oyston, E. (ed.) (2003) *Centred on Learning: academic case studies on learning centre development*, Aldershot, Ashgate.

Organizations

British Universities Film and Video Council (BUFVC),
www.bufvc.ac.uk [accessed 23 December 2004].

Educational Recording Agency (ERA),
www.era.org.uk [accessed 23 December 2004].

Higher Education Funding Council for England and Wales (HEFCE),
www.hefce.ac.uk [accessed 23 December 2004].

IPR Helpdesk,
www.ipr-helpdesk.org [accessed 23 December 2004].

Joint Information Systems Committee (JISC),
www.jisc.ac.uk [accessed 23 December 2004].

Universities UK (UUK),
www.universitiesuk.ac.uk [accessed 23 December 2004].

5   The corporate rights holder's perspective

Ian Watson

Introduction

As noted in previous chapters digital rights management can mean different things. On the one hand it can refer to back-office processes and procedures for tracking rights negotiations and licences awarded; on the other, it can mean technological systems for physically preventing access to and copying of protected works.

In the pre-digital age, copyright regulated the distribution and multiplication of works, but it did not try to regulate consumption, mainly because it did not have to. The business model of the rights holder was not threatened by the consumption of, for example, books. In contrast, the ease with which digital media can be distributed and multiplied presents digital rights holders with a dilemma because they perceive a threat to their revenue if one purchased copy can be replicated perfectly and endlessly.

A basic tenet of DRM is that the rights holder, or controller, should be able to exercise control over who can do what to a piece of content and for what sum of money or other consideration. One of the problems facing the corporate rights holder is the difficulty of untangling what can be quite a complicated mix of ownership and second-use rights. Indeed it is not uncommon to find that ownership is ill defined.

This chapter considers the perspective of the corporate rights holder in general, drawing on the specific case of the newspaper publisher. After examining the 'back office' aspects of DRM, attention turns to the debate on the legitimacy of anti-circumvention devices and how the corporate rights holder might approach a future in which the whole question of the relevancy of copyright to digital assets is being questioned.

As far as the back-office processes are concerned the corporate rights holder is involved in:

- verifying who owns copyright
- negotiating third-party rights
- agreeing fees
- tracking usage
- prevention of piracy or other illegal use.

The rights process, whether digital or analogue, has two parts:

- granting a rights licence
- agreeing the fee, which may be nil, or another consideration, for example a credit.

Having established the ownership status of a piece of content the corporate rights holder is faced with the task of preventing illegal use, which can be difficult in the digital environment. Many rights holders, particularly in the entertainment industries, have adopted technological measures aimed at controlling use. The other contributors have considered the impact of these technological measures on legitimate use. This chapter considers the extent to which such measures do in fact provide a viable business model for the digital age.

Economic and moral rights

Reuse of content (articles, photographs, cartoons, etc.), whether in electronic editions of the printed newspaper or by third parties, requires clarity with respect to the ownership of copyright and moral rights attached to the original work.

Verifying ownership

To take print publishers – and newspapers in particular – as an example, the production workflow often records very little

information about the rights status of the elements – text, photographs, cartoons, maps, charts and diagrams – that make up the page. These elements are usually obtained from many sources, including news agencies, specialist graphics suppliers and freelance writers and photographers. While these digital objects may have contained information about rights as metadata when they first entered in the workflow, by the time they have been incorporated into the printed page this information may be either lost or not readily available.

Rosenblatt, Trippe and Mooney (2002) explain how the production process for electronic products (whether books, compact disks or videos) should deliver two things:

- a finished product in the format the market requires
- metadata for catalogues and e-commerce systems.

The problem for a traditional publisher of books or newspapers who wishes to repurpose content for electronic markets is that the workflow is probably based on a desktop publishing system such as QuarkXpress which, although well suited to producing printed output, does not necessarily seamlessly produce an electronic product. Even though it may be relatively simple to produce an electronic output as a pdf (Adobe's portable document format), it is highly likely that the metadata describing the ownership and rights attached to each object will be lost.

This kind of workflow tends to be ill suited to the task of integration with a DRM solution. According to Rosenblatt, a digital asset management system (DAM) is often required before a DRM system. In other words, a system is needed to manage all the materials, whether in digital or analogue form, that go into the final product. These materials can include photographs, diagrams, commissioned articles, video clips, sound files and so on.

The whole workflow has to be analysed so that a DAM system can properly record ownership and rights information about digital objects as soon as they enter the workflow or as soon as they are digitized. This might seem obvious but changing workflows and work practices can be difficult and, in practical terms, require liaison between the various departments that have a stake in the production and contractual processes: editorial, legal, personnel and marketing.

The introduction of a digital photography system to a newspaper, for example, requires photographers and imaging operatives to learn a new set of disciplines. As soon as a photograph is downloaded from camera to desktop, or scanned from a hard copy, at a minimum the following information must be recorded:

- name of photographer
- owner of copyright (not necessarily the same as above)
- subject matter: who, what's happening, where, when.

To record copyright ownership accurately it is necessary to know the employment status of the photographer: those who are employees will normally have assigned their copyright to the employer; photographers who are freelance are unlikely to have assigned copyright.

It is then necessary to record any special payment details, such as 'free first use'; 'pay on second use'; or 'may not be used again without written permission'.

Repurposing

Newspapers have been around for more than 200 years and have become very good at aggregating content from all kinds of sources into the familiar printed tabloid or broadsheet format. The arrival of electronic archives in the 1980s did not cause much of a ripple mainly because the high cost of access to online archives hosted by the likes of Dialog, Lexis Nexis and their predecessors meant they were largely unknown outside the business and academic worlds. The arrival of the world wide web (WWW) along with cheap desktop computers opened up this exclusive world to a much wider audience. With this increased visibility came a growing awareness of the scope for illegal copying. Newspapers put their content on the web and saw it copied without permission. Freelance contributors and news agencies such as Reuters and the Press Association equally cried foul if their copy started appearing on newspapers' web editions without explicit agreement. The contractual arrangements between the publishers and contributors (freelance or agency) usually related exclusively to the printed product and did not cater for the arrival of what some might argue was simply 'electronic extensions' of the printed product. The publisher wishing to diversify into digital media was therefore faced with contract renegotiation and possible additional costs.

Freelance contributors

Freelance writers and photographers retain their copyright unless they explicitly assign it to the publisher. This is an area in which contract and copyright law interact and the corporate rights holder needs to be mindful of the nature of the agreement with the freelancer. Publishers have been accused of 'rights grabbing' (see, for example, Bently, 2002) when they sought to secure the rights to include freelance material in electronic media which, as suggested above, could be seen as extensions of the printed product, for example online editions, CD-ROM archives and online databases.

In the mid-1990s Jonathan Tasini, President of the National Writers' Union in the USA, challenged the right of newspapers to publish freelance copy in any other medium other than the printed page without express agreement. The freelancers' argument was that they had sold to the publisher First Serial Rights only: the right to publish the article once only. The publishers argued, unsuccessfully it turned out, that by securing First Serial Rights from the freelance writers they had secured implied rights for electronic republication. This, they argued, was an electronic extension of the printed publication, not a new publication.

In June 2001, the United States Supreme Court found in favour of Tasini (Supreme Court of the United States, New York Times Co., Inc., et al. vs Tasini et al., No 00-201, decided June 2001, www.supremecourtus.gov/opinions/00slipopinion.html.) The case has had an enormous impact in the USA and beyond, resulting in freelance copy being excised from the archives of online vendors such as Lexis Nexis and Factiva.

While hailed as a victory for freelancers, some expressed the view that this rendered them invisible to prospective employers because their work was no longer included in the public record (except of course in hard copies and microfilm held in libraries). Others legitimately responded that, while there was undoubtedly benefit to them of having their material in the archives, they were nonetheless entitled to a share of any financial benefit accruing to the publisher. The exclusion of freelance copy from 'electronic extensions' of printed works does not, it could be argued, serve the interests of any of the three parties (freelance creator, publisher or the public) to the copyright bargain.

As newspapers aggregate material from many sources, a contractual regime is required in which a film review, for example, can appear in the electronic archive regardless of whether it was created by a staff or a freelance writer. This serves the interests of the customer who cares little about the contractual status of the writer. Historic archives riddled with holes will poorly serve future generations of scholars. Worse, in many cases there is no record that a hole exists because generally there is no marker in online archives to say that content has been removed. The argument could go on forever. The answer lies in a contract, a very useful legal device for specifying what may or may not be done with the work and the relevant financial arrangements.

The onus is therefore on the publisher and the writers to reach contractual arrangements which meet the need of all parties. *The Guardian* newspaper took a step in this direction in the late 1990s when it devised an Online Charter (www.guardian.co.uk/guardian/article/0,5814,409883,00.html), clearly setting out the rights and obligations of the newspaper and its freelance contributors. With reference to copyright, the charter states the agreed terms on which *The Guardian* accepts freelance contributions. The key elements of these terms are:

- rights of use in all editions in paper form, including editions printed overseas
- non-exclusive electronic database rights, e.g. CD-ROM archives, websites, online databases
- syndication rights for one year
- rights to license the photocopying of cuttings for customers' internal information purposes.

Crucially the charter goes on to specify the remuneration arrangements that are attached to these terms. Many would regard this as a sensible set of guidelines that provides a clear basis for negotiation.

PDF editions

Adobe's portable document format (PDF) has become an important output and distribution format for all kinds of publisher. The file size of a newspaper page in PDF can be relatively small, a factor which contributes to its portability and offers the advantage that pages can be routed very easily to alternative printing sites anywhere in the world. PDF also allows for exact page replication of the hard copy, thus protecting the integrity of the content so that the reader can see exactly how the story appeared in the original hard-copy version, including its position, prominence and typographical characteristics.

More importantly for the current discussion is that PDFs can be delivered to personal computers around the world at virtually no cost. The cost of sending a printed broadsheet newspaper from the UK to Canada can be up to ten times the retail price, which would make it economically ruinous for even the most well heeled ex-patriots to keep up to date with news from home. PDF offers a solution, but gives rise to some problems.

One might ask what is the difference between a PDF displayed on my laptop while sunning myself on the Costa del Sol and a newspaper printed locally from that same PDF. Well, the publisher owns copyright in the page (its design and layout) but may not own copyright in the individual elements on the page, for example cartoons and photographs.

The question of whether a PDF edition is an extension of the printed product is controversial. In December 2003, the UK Audit Bureau of Circulation (ABC) (www.journalism.co.uk/news/story813.shtml) announced that publishers could include digital editions on the ABC certificate as they are the 'same product' as the print edition. The ABC certificate is of vital importance to the publisher because it provides the independent evidence of the number of copies sold, required to support advertising rates. As print circulation falls and is, to some extent, replaced by electronic versions the latter become increasingly important.

The Association of Online Publishers takes the view that:

> . . . although delivered through the internet, digital publications are simply an additional delivery format for the print publication . . .[and] should be

treated in the same way as the recent compact editions of broadsheet
newspapers.   www.journalism.co.uk/news/story813.shtml

Some publishers take the view that this supports the argument that
the price paid for, say, a photograph includes use in both print and
digital editions since they are the same product. The British
Association of Picture Libraries and Agencies (BAPLA) has
questioned this view and is seeking clarification.

Whatever the outcome, the solution must ensure that the publisher
can make use of new and convenient media and that the reader can
enjoy a newspaper or magazine in either print or digital form. The
reader also demands access to back copies, the printing and storage of
which are expensive: PDF offers a convenient method of storage and
delivery. This reinforces the importance of the contractual
arrangements under which the publisher secures the rights necessary
to meet its obligations to its readers. That obligation includes
delivering a representation of the original publication as faithfully and
economically as possible.

Newspaper Licensing Agency

A problem facing many corporate rights holders is that collecting
royalties is not their core business. Rosenblatt (2002) observes that
aggregation is the key to economic viability and that the DRM
collecting societies such as the American Society of Composers,
Authors and Publishers (ASCAP) and CCC in the USA have become
market-makers by collecting royalties that were uneconomic for the
rights holder to collect and for the rights user to pay.

Established in January 1996, the NLA is a collecting society which
sells licences to organizations allowing them to make photocopies of
individual articles from newspapers. Before the existence of the NLA,
newspaper publishers were faced with the difficulty and administrative
overhead of collecting small sums of money from a large number of
sources. Businesses and educational establishments wishing to make
copies for commercial or educational purposed were faced with the
overhead of seeking permission on each and every occasion, while the
rights holder faced the overhead of checking the copyright status of
each article and negotiating a fee.

In this situation the transaction costs are likely to exceed the likely royalty receivable. The NLA, like all collecting societies, has been successful in reducing the transaction costs by focusing on the management of rights in a specific business area. Both the rights owner and the user benefit from greater clarity of what is allowed and what is not and from a simple payment system.

The newspaper, however, does not own the copyright of all that it publishes. In order to ensure that freelance contributors receive a share of the revenue accruing from copying, the NLA undertakes periodic sample surveys to determine the proportion of material photocopied from each newspaper that is attributable to freelance contributors. The newspaper publisher is required to submit to the NLA lists of its regular freelance contributors and news agencies. Over a specified period the NLA monitors what is copied and determines the proportion of royalty revenue that should be returned by the publisher (the rights holder) to the freelance contributors. Random checks ensure that the publishers' information is correct. The net effect is that both freelance contributors and the newspaper publishers receive revenue that was previously uneconomic to collect. The NLA, like the Copyright Licensing Agency, has attempted to extend this model to digital rights, to provide a simple way for the rights holder to collect revenue for the use of content in electronic media such as websites. At the time of writing the impact of these initiatives has been limited, leaving the onus on the rights holder and prospective user to negotiate rights for digital use case by case, the administrative costs of which tend to outweigh revenue.

Archives and contempt of court

The corporate rights holder must be aware of the legal status of online archives.

Archives as continuous publications

In a Scottish court case the judge ruled that material held in an electronic archive and retrievable via a web browser was an act of publication just as much as printing the story in the newspaper (High Court of Justiciary, Opinion (No2), The Right Honourable Lord

Osborne *In Causa* Her Majesty's Advocate against William Frederick
Ian Beggs, www.scotcourts. gov.uk/opinionsv/osb1910.htm). This
suggests that the online electronic archives which are licensed to
aggregators such as Lexis Nexis, Dialog, etc. may in effect be seen as
one huge, continuous publication.

Every edition of a newspaper is subject to a process known as
'legalling', in which a lawyer gives instant advice on any legal matter
that might arise from publication. The lawyer will be aware of any
current court cases that might make publication of a particular story
an act of contempt of court. Thus, in Her Majesty's Advocate vs
William Frederick Ian Beggs, it was argued that the existence of a
story in an archive describing the history of the defendant amounted
to contempt of court just as much as if the story had been published
while proceedings were active. The judge agreed that press reports
concerning the accused had potentially damaged his chances of a fair
trial:

> Furthermore, a cause for concern was the fact that much of the
> published material . . . remained available for public scrutiny on a
> number of websites on the internet. Some of this material took the form
> of the archives of national newspapers and broadcasting organizations.

Turning to the question of whether an electronic version of a story
was different from its printed cousin the judge took the view that:

> . . . newspapers quite legitimately published the material involved at a
> time when that act was not objectionable. That published material had
> been made available in electronic form and remained available at a time
> when its contents were objectionable. Thus the attempt to argue that the
> material had become part of an archive and hence was not being
> published, was without substance.

The judge, however, concluded that there had been no contempt of
court:

> It appears to me that the availability of the material as part of an archive,
> as opposed to part of a current publication renders it less likely that it
> may come to the attention of a juror than would be the case if it formed

part of a contemporaneous publication. Furthermore . . . the material concerned would not be likely to be accessed by the insertion of the name . . . in a search engine. In order to access it, it would be necessary to obtain access to the Website of the newspaper, or other publication which contained the material. Thus, an individual undertaking a random search . . . would not be likely to access the material.

Archives and the one-year limitation rule

Two other relevant cases are those of Loutchansky vs Times Newspapers Limited and Dow Jones and Co. Inc. vs Gutnik (see www.kevinboone.com/PF_gutnick.html and www.lawreports.co.uk/civdecb0.2.htm).

In the Loutchansky case *The Times* newspaper had alleged in the printed newspaper and on its website that one Mr Loutchansky was involved in criminal activity. The court concluded that information published on the website, unlike information printed in a newspaper, was not subject to the one-year limitation rule (an action for defamation must be brought within one year of publication). The reasoning for this decision seemed to be that each time the defamatory statement was transferred from *The Times* web server to a reader's browser, this constituted a separate act of publication. Thus a claim for defamation could never become time barred: a story published ten years ago could still be the subject of a defamation claim.

The Court of Appeal stressed the need for `responsible journalism', asserting that, whenever new facts about a case come to light, web publishers must review everything available on their web servers in the light of these new facts, and amend as appropriate. If newspapers were to excise material from their archives every time a case came to court they would have to subject their archives to a continuous process of legal scrutiny. Apart from the practical difficulties this could be an expensive process.

Archives and the relevant jurisdiction

The Gutnick case concerned an article published in the online version of *Barrons Magazine*, which is owned by Dow Jones, an American company with its web server located in the USA. The article alleged that Mr Gutnick, an Australian citizen, was a scoundrel. When Mr Gutnick lodged a suit for defamation in Australia, Dow Jones contended that Australian courts did not have jurisdiction to hear the case.

Different countries have settled on different places to draw the line between freedom of expression and defamation. In Australia and the UK, the line tends to give priority to protection from defamation; in the USA, the boundary tends to favour freedom of speech. A person defending a claim for defamation is likely, therefore, to prefer the USA to Australia or the UK.

Echoing the Loutchansky case the Australian courts took the view that `publication' took place at the time and place where the offending article became available on the reader's web browser, not when it was posted on the Dow Jones web server. The case could therefore be heard in an Australian court. The point of interest in this case is that a publication made in the USA by a US company was deemed to be actionable in Australia. The corporate rights owner must be mindful that an article posted on a web server in the UK could result in legal action almost anywhere in the world. Defamation is therefore a matter of some concern for the digital rights holder.

The Law Commissioner's view

Mindful of such concerns, the Law Commission published the results of its investigation into the potential problems with the way the law of defamation and contempt of court affected internet communications (Law Commission, 2002). The report highlights four areas of concern:

- the liability of internet service providers (ISPs) for other people's material
- the application of the limitation period to online archives
- the exposure of internet publishers to liability in other jurisdictions
- the risk of prosecution for contempt of court.

Although there has as yet been no official response to the report it is worth noting that the Law Commission recognized the potentially damaging impact of removing any limitation period for actions against electronic publications:

> We recommend a review of the way in which each download from an online archive gives rise to a fresh cause of action, and causes the limitation period to begin anew . . . it is potentially unfair to defendants to allow actions to be brought against archive-holders many years after the original publication . . . . Online archives have a social utility, and it would not be desirable to hinder their development.

On jurisdiction and applicable law, the Law Commission noted the concerns of publishers who faced unacceptable levels of global risks as well as those of claimants who felt they should be able seek redress in the country to which the damage to their reputation had taken place. The Commission's conclusion offers little comfort to the corporate rights holder for the time being:

> Although we have some sympathy with the concerns expressed about 'unacceptable levels of global risks', any solution would require an international treaty, accompanied by greater harmonisation of the substantive law of defamation. We do not think that the problem can be solved within the short to medium term. We do not therefore recommend reform in this area at the present time.

Regarding contempt of court, the Commission placed faith in the criminal justice system, providing some comfort to the rights holder with material in online archives:

> We accept that it is not practically possible to monitor all criminal trials in the country and subsequently remove from internet archives any potentially prejudicial material. Jurors cannot be prevented from using the internet to search for detrimental material on criminal defendants if they are determined to do so.
>
> However, the criminal justice system places trust in the good sense of jurors to decide cases on the evidence before them. Although in theory it is possible that contempt of court law could be applied inappropriately to an 'unwitting' defendant, we think that there are already sufficient safeguards in the existing law to ensure that internet publishers are

protected against inappropriate, arbitrary or trivial prosecution. We do not consider this area to be a priority for law reform.

Digital rights licensing

The rights holder should define specifically what is being licensed, to whom and for how long.

Define content to be licensed

This might seem obvious but it is important to define how much content is required. In the case of a newspaper publisher the elements that might be licensed include:

* headline
* headline and text
* accompanying photograph or other graphical material
* the entire text or an edited version.

Requests for edited versions should be treated with caution, not least because editing could infringe the moral rights of the creator. The rights holder should always exercise a veto over editing.

Geographical extent

The client should also give an indication of the geographic extent of the rights sought. For example, if an extract from an article is to be used in a television production, the fee will be dependent upon whether the production is to be released in the UK or worldwide. In the online digital world, geographic limitations become problematic.

Doctorow (2004) makes a valid argument that copyright law should have no geographic dimension. Specifically he complains about the regional codes that are attached to films released on digital versatile disc (DVD), which prevent the purchaser of a DVD playing it in a region other than the one in which it was purchased. In his view the purchaser owns the physical object (the film industry does in fact use the advertising line 'own it on DVD') and should not be prevented from playing it anywhere in the world, in the same way that there is no legal barrier to taking a book anywhere in the world. This is a compelling argument, which challenges the anti-circumvention provisions of EU and US copyright law.

For the purposes of the current discussion, however, the rights holder can legitimately specify a geographic dimension as part of an assessment of the extent to which the prospective buyer intends to exploit the asset. In the same way that book publishers may acquire rights to publish only in certain countries, so the holder of the copyright of a photograph may vary the fee according to the number of countries in which the buyer wishes to sell his final product. The rights holder is placing no restrictions on the final consumer of the product in which his digital asset in embodied. They are simply measuring the extent to which their asset will be used. Put another way, the world market is bigger that the EU market which is bigger than the UK market. The rights holder has a reasonable economic argument for bargaining on the basis of market for the finished product. Whether or not it is acceptable for the seller of that product to use technological means to prevent its use in certain geographic areas is another argument which will be returned to later.

Duration

It is wise to impose a time limit, otherwise the client may use the material forever. Circumstances may change and the rights holder may wish to reassert control. In the case of a website it may be advisable to limit permission to one year, or even six months. For books it is usual to issue permission for a specific edition. The digital equivalent might be for a specific period.

Deep linking vs content licensing

In the mid-1990s *The Shetland Times* obtained an interim interdict (injunction in English law) to stop *The Shetland News* from publishing deep links to content on its (*The Shetland Times*) website. The *Times* argued that its content was displayed on the *News* website as if it were the content of the *News* and that readers would not be directed to the home page of the *Times*, thereby depriving its advertisers of the all-important 'eyeballs'.

This case was settled out of court but it focused attention on the question of deep linking. Under the terms of the settlement, the *News* was not allowed to create deep links to the *Times*. Instead, the link was to be to the front page of the *Times* and the headlines that appeared on the *News* website had to appear on a page which included the legend 'A Shetland Times Story' in the same size or larger than the corresponding legend of the *News*. (For a chronology see www.lectlaw.com/files/elw10.htm and for summary of the interdict and settlement see ww.lectlaw.com/files/elw10.htm.)

Since then the design of websites has developed considerably and it is possible to allow deep linking in a way that ensures the article is displayed in context. Sometimes it is wise to suggest a deep link rather than a licence to reproduce on a third-party website. An important condition to impose is that the story must not be displayed within a frame on the licensee's site because this might constitute passing off. Deep linking might be regarded as a digital citation. There is little substantive difference between a reader of this chapter transcribing one of the URL citations into a browser and a reader of a digital version clicking a hyperlink.

Product endorsement/derogatory treatment

The web is an excellent medium for campaigning groups and it is not uncommon for such groups to include press comment favourable to their causes. This material adds value to the website, but it is common to encounter reluctance to pay for this content.

The corporate rights holder must take care to avoid unintended endorsement of a cause or product. If a newspaper publishes an article favourably reviewing a particular product, the owner of that product may be interested in using the article, or part of it, to promote the product (a use which, incidentally, is not covered by a licence from the Newspaper Licensing Agency). It is wise to check exactly how this information is to be presented and that the manner of presentation does not give a false impression of the tenor of the original article. The same applies to websites established by individual people or pressure groups. Allowing the reproduction of articles on the site may be construed as endorsement of the cause and the better option may be to allow a hyperlink from the headline back to the rights holder's own site. The concern can be illustrated in the world of arts and entertainment where quotations from reviewers are frequently reproduced on book covers or posters for theatrical productions in a very selective way, often out of context.

Agreeing the fee

The price for a digital asset is usually agreed through negotiation in order to arrive at a price that reflects the value of the object to the licensee and the value of the object to the rights holder. As in the analogue world, the corporate rights holder will try to measure the importance, or value, of the object to the licensee's proposed use.

The British Association of Picture Libraries and Agencies (BAPLA at www.bapla.org) makes available to its members extensive and detailed guidance on how to price photographs for use in traditional media as well as electronic, including websites, intranets, CD-ROMs and DVDs. This guidance is based upon surveys of the range of fees negotiated by its members. The fee for websites could take account of the number of hits and the manner in which the photograph is to be used, for example as a navigation button, on the home page, on a menu or as part of the body of the site.

Waiving the fee

Rights holders are often asked to waive fees for all kinds of reasons. The same rules that apply to the analogue world are relevant for digital content. The rights holder should be clear as to the reason for waiving the fee. Charities and educational publishers should not automatically expect discounts or free use: the rights holder is entitled to decide which charities it chooses to support.

There are occasions when it is of benefit to both parties to waive the fee. The corporate rights holders may have to ensure co-ordination between the rights department and the marketing department. For example, a television production company wishes to use digitized images of newspaper pages as a background set-dressing for a studio discussion. While a fee could be negotiated it is also conceivable that the rights holder (the newspaper publisher) might derive value from brand exposure every time the TV programme is broadcast. Weighing that value against the value to the TV programme of an interesting and topical set is ultimately a matter of negotiation and relative bargaining strength. This is perhaps one example where waiving the fee serves the needs of all parties, including the viewer.

Record keeping and enforcement
Manual recording

Keeping a record of what rights have been licensed and to whom is essential. This need not be a sophisticated system and a spreadsheet might be adequate. When an enquiry is received an entry is made to record what is being sought along with details of the preliminary negotiations. The minimum data to record are:

- date of enquiry
- name and contact details of enquirer
- description of digital objects
- rights sought, including geographic and time factors
- fee agreed/invoiced/paid.

While a spreadsheet may be adequate for this purpose, it can become unwieldy and it might be preferable to migrate to a database such as Microsoft Access in order to allow for more complex operations such as searching and reporting by expiry date, and so on.

Automated systems

This kind of operation is labour intensive. Consideration might be given to a technology-based system that will automatically conclude the transaction. As Rosenblatt (2002) notes, most rights and permission departments operate in a rather chaotic fashion, mainly because of the difficulty of subjecting the process to a well defined set of rules. Highly valuable properties, such as the film rights to a novel, will be negotiated at an individual level, and usually at a high level. This high-value level of transaction would not be suitable for a rights management system.

At the other end of the scale, Rosenblatt observes that no two publishers handle rights and permissions the same way, which makes it difficult for the DRM system vendor to create a product that is suitable for more than a handful of publishers. The implication is that the cost of implementing a DRM system could be more than the expected financial return.

Technological solutions such as Info2clear (www.info2clear.com) offer content creators an infrastructure for online copyright clearance and sale of reproduction rights. For example, Info2clear's Get-a-seal is an online digital notary which allows authors, photographers and other content creators to obtain a digitally signed, time-stamped copyright registration for their content. Such registration can be used as evidence in case of copyright dispute.

This kind of system is costly to install and maintain and the publisher is faced with the question of whether it is worth pursuing a royalty when the royalty itself is far less than the cost of collection.

Reuters, one of the world's leading news agencies, has employed a software system to monitor the web for republication and copyright infringement of its news content. The system has been designed to identify instances where a party goes beyond fair use by copying a full story without licence or deriving a story from Reuters content without acknowledgement. Reuters is not concerned about quotes included on weblogs or on other news sites that link to the original material. The system will, according to Reuters, allow it to monitor which news stories are the most popular and ensure the company is 'producing enough of the right material, keeping in touch with what the market wants'. The company also uses video watermarking to mark video content, and plans to develop additional tools that will allow it to track unauthorized use of photographs (www.internetnews.com/bus-news/article.php/3330381).

Digital object identifier (DOI)

In 1994 the Association of American Publishers came up with the idea of a digital object identifier to uniquely identify any digital object, whether a learned article, a movie clip or a piece of music. It is possible to include with a DOI an existing identifier from the analogue works, e.g. an ISBN or ISSN. See www.doi.org/index.html

for more information about the digital object identifier system.
According to Electronic Publishing Services (2004), DOIs have not yet
been implemented within encryption-based DRM systems. If unique
identifiers for content become widely used in publishing they could
provide a hook on which to hang rights management.

Business models

Rosenblatt (2002) argues that by concentrating on copyright
protection early DRM solutions failed to address the question of
developing viable business models. DRM works, he believes, only
where it supports the business model rather than the other way
round. The corporate rights holder has a variety of models to choose
from, including:

- paid download
- subscriptions
- pay-per-view
- usage metering
- selling rights.

The most suitable model will depend on the type of content on offer
and the characteristics of the customer. A successful DRM system that
delivers content to a user depends on a carefully planned model.

According to Electronic Publishing Services (2004), the technology
companies promoting DRM systems have failed to understand the
publishing business, its business models and how DRM could support
these models. DRM systems can help in the following ways:

- limiting copyright infringement
- creating a mix of business models, including setting expiry dates
  and quotas for individual users
- tracking data use.

The recorded music industry has, however, had a difficult time
coming to terms with digital distribution. Alderman (2001) catalogues
the tortuous paths taken by the music industry to find a business
model for digital music that dovetailed with the existing systems for

distributing recorded music. While the main players experimented
with formats and business models, trying to come to terms with the
MP3 music compression standard and digital music providers such as
Liquid Audio, along came Napster, the creation of a bored student
who simply wanted to share music with his peers. Napster was
effectively a directory of music files held on the computers of its
subscribers. A subscriber could look up a song title and be offered a
list of computers from which it could be downloaded. It would be fair
to say that Napster caused panic, but its instant popularity sprang
from its ability to deliver what the customer wanted, The problem for
Napster, of course, was that is was not founded on a carefully
considered business model because what it was doing was illegal.
Nonetheless, it could be argued that Napster was at least partly
responsible for prompting the music business to think more creatively
about meeting consumer demand for digital music.

It has been suggested that rights holders throughout the 20th
century had a very poor track record in evolving business models that
coped with technical change (see Doctorow, 2004; Thierer and Crews,
2002; Litman, 2001). At the end of the 19th century the music
industry was mostly concerned with selling sheet music. This model
was challenged when, in the 1870s, Henri Furneaux invented the
'player piano' which recorded music onto punched tape as the pianist
played the music. The punched tape could be duplicated and played
back any number of times on other machines (see Lessig, 2002). The
sheet-music publishers were extremely unhappy and, according to
Doctorow (2004), the American composer Sousa submitted to
Congress that:

> These talking machines are going to ruin the artistic development of
> music in this country . . . the vocal chord will be eliminated by a process
> of evolution as was the tail of man when he came from the ape.

Like so many predictions of the dire consequences for the established
order of adopting new technologies, this one has proved to be
spectacularly wide of the mark. Congress decided that the best way to
ensure fairness and technological development was to introduce a
compulsory licensing system so that anyone could make a piano roll
provided they paid the publisher a fee fixed by Congress.

This licence created a world where:

> . . . a thousand times more money was made by a thousand times more creators who made a thousand times more music that reached a thousand times more people.
>
> Doctorow, 2004

Litman (2001) has documented how the various established interests negotiated amendments to the copyright law throughout the 20th century to hinder 'upstart' industries such as radio and television, which were perceived as threats to their business models:

> Negotiated privileges [to copy or protect rights] tend to be very specific, and pose substantial entry barriers to outsiders who can't be at the negotiating table because their industries haven't been invented yet. So negotiated copyright statutes have tended, throughout the century, to be kind to the entrenched status quo and hostile to upstart new industries.

Thus, in 1982 the US film industry sought to prevent Sony launching its Betamax video cassette recorder (VCR). Ruling against the vested interests of Hollywood Congress did not mince its words:

> If your business model can't survive the emergence of this general-purpose tool, it's time to get another business-model or go broke.
>
> Doctorow, 2004

The lesson is that new media do not succeed by trying to be like old media, only better. They succeed because 'they're worse than old media at the stuff old media is good at, and better at the stuff old media are bad at' (Doctorow, 2004).

Doctorow argues strongly that to abandon invention is to rob tomorrow's artists of the new businesses and audiences that the internet and the PC can give them. The challenge for the rights holder is to find a model that allows this to happen.

The circumvention of anti-circumvention devices is now illegal under both US and EU law. The question that rights holders have to answer is whether employing anti-circumvention devices will in fact grow their business in the long run. Is it legitimate, for example, to disable the fast forward function through the copyright warning at the

beginning of a DVD? Should the 'owner' of the DVD be forced to read it every time it is viewed?

Summary

DRM may ultimately be seen less as a copyright infringement protection tool than as a facilitator for new business models, and it is here that the true value lies for content publishers (Electronic Publishing Services, 2004). DRM will allow publishers to track usage in a way that overcomes the current problems of negotiating and collecting low-value transactions. If it takes an hour of negotiation to agree a fee of £60 the publisher is likely to hit the 'why bother' barrier. It is possible that digital object identifiers (DOI) might become more widespread as a tool for DRM.

The Commission of the European Communities (2004) notes that DRM systems and services will benefit both rights holders and consumers only if such systems can simultaneously protect the interests of the former while easing access for the latter. This might be easier said than done. At present, it is argued, DRM systems do not ensure an appropriate balance between all the interested parties.

On the other hand, Rosenblatt (2002) takes the view that publishers could improve their status by the mere act of employing DRM:

> Rights management systems will help rights holders who maintain trusted sources of content . . . communicate to customers that their content is of value. The mere act of going to the effort and expense of adopting rights management systems . . . says something to customers about your commitment to product quality. Saying that you care about controlling rights goes a long way toward differentiating your products from a product from a company who doesn't care about rights.

The challenge for the corporate rights holder is to avoid the rather Luddite approach that characterized reaction to new technology throughout the last century. DRM models must not prevent legitimate access to and use of legitimately acquired digital assets. Hausman (2002), the CEO of CentreSpan Communications Corporation, argues for a middle way between the copyright anarchists who preach a doctrine of infringement and the copyright maximalists who appear to be eliminating traditional fair use concepts through the use of heavy-handed technological barriers. He makes the important observation that the middle way should be firmly grounded in clarifying and protecting the rights of consumers:

> The digital media distribution business is a consumer service business and failing to meet the legitimate expectation of consumers will inevitably lead to the failure of digital media ventures.

The 'first sale' doctrine is not meaningful or applicable in the digital environment, mainly because the seller of a 'used' digital file can retain a perfect digital copy for continued use. The challenge for corporate digital rights holders is to develop business models that give the consumers of digital products the convenience of the first sale doctrine.

References

Alderman, J. (2001) *Sonic Boom: Napster, P2P and the future of music*, London, Fourth Estate.

Bently, L. (2002) *Between a Rock and a Hard Place: the problems facing freelance creators in the UK media market-place*, London, Institute of Employment Rights.

Commission of the European Communities (2004) *The Management of Copyright and Related Rights in the Internal Market*, Communication from the Commission to the Council, The European Parliament and the European Economic and Social Committee, COM (2004) 261 final.

Doctorow, C. (2004) Microsoft Research DRM talk, delivered to Microsoft's Research Group, 17 June.

Electronic Publishing Services (2004) *Digital Rights Management: gaining real value from implementation*, www.epsltd.com [accessed 23 December 2004].

Hausman, F. G. (2002) Protecting Intellectual Property in the Digital Age. In Thierer, A. et al. (eds) *Copy Fights*, Washington, Cato Institute.

Law Commission (2002) *Defamation and the Internet: a preliminary investigation*, www.lawcom.gov.uk/files/defamation2.pdf [accessed

23 December 2004].

Lessig, L. (2002) *The Future of Ideas: the fate of the commons in a connected world*, New York, Vintage Books.

Litman, J. (2001) *Digital Copyright*, Amherst, Prometheus Books.

Lloyd, I. (2000) *Information Technology Law*, London, Butterworths.

Rosenblatt, B., Trippe, B. and Mooney, S. (2002) *Digital Rights Management Business and Technology*, M&T Books.

Thierer, A. and Crews, W. (eds) (2002) *Copy Fights*, Washington, Cato Institute.

Index